#INSPIRATION101

think like an entrepreneur, act like a prostitute

Tumisang Tsolope
19/FEB/18

GOITSEMANG J. KHUTSAFALO

PUBLISHED BY: GOITSEMANG J. KHUTSAFALO

Think like an Entrepreneur, Act like a Prostitute

ISBN: 978-99968-0-668-1

Published in Botswana by:

Goitsemang J. Khutsafalo

For further information or permission, address:

Goitsemang J. Khutsafalo

The Office Building, Plot 64517, Fairgrounds

Gaborone, Botswana

Tel: (+267) 77 045 403

Visit: www.launchitinternational.com

Printed in South Africa by: Hartwood Digital Printers

Most quotations were taken from random Google searches, unless specified.

TABLE OF CONTENTS

DEDICATIONS

As the saying goes, *"From the smallest families of the smallest villages often comes the greatest of the greatest"*, this book is dedicated to every young person out there whom despite where they are coming from and what they are going through are still willing to pursue their dreams which will one day shake the world. If your inside tells you that you were born to influence the world, if you feel within you that you were born to join the league of the world's greatest entrepreneurs, if you feel within you that your local community is too small for your greatness, if you feel that your name should one day be listed among the great names on the Forbes Billionaires & Millionaires, I want you to know that your dreams are relevant, and I would like to personally dedicate this book to you.

I would like to lastly dedicate this book to every special person out there who is willing to be used by God to change millions and billions of lives across all the surface areas of the world in this generation.

ACKNOWLEDGEMENTS

I have always thought that writing a book is a simple thing to do. I always thought that all you do is just 'type'. But writing this book has proven me wrong in many ways. It has been a great experience and a great learning curve for me writing this great book. It helped me to meet awesome people, learn from the great as well as get their assistance in putting this book together. It will be wrong for me to not express my sincere gratitude towards them. Firstly, I want to thank *Moemedi Motseothata* for agreeing to sell me his tablet which has been a great blessing to me in writing this book in the most flexible way possible. It is through this tablet that I was able to write this book during my long travels, seminars and almost every free time I could come across. I should thank everyone who invited me to speak at their workshops and seminars during the period of writing this book, it gave me the opportunity to share the contents of this book with different audiences and get feedback which produced some chapters of this book.

I would like to thank everyone who have for the past five years been asking about *"when are you writing your first book?"*. This question has been a great motivation to me. I'm not planning on dying with any of my dreams, this book has been one of those dreams, that's why I want to thank God for having given me yet another opportunity to achieve one of my dreams. I want to thank God and give him the glory that he deserves for giving me the idea of this book as well as insights and revelations documented in this great book. Thank you Lord for your grace sponsorship that has made this book one of the greatest books ever written in the continent of Africa on entrepreneurship. Only you and I understand better. You are indeed a great God, there's none like thee our Lord Jesus Christ.

PREFACE

What an amazing time to be alive today, did you know that many of these businesses that are worth billions today didn't even exist a couple of years ago? There has never been the right time or should I say the best time on this planet to be an entrepreneur than today. Do you know why? Because barriers of entry into the business world are dropping every single day. You can be in the village and build something that will worth a couple of billions in a couple of years to come. I think for that very reason you should realize how blessed you are to be alive at this time on planet earth. In the past, for you to get into the newspaper business you had to spend so much money in signing publishing and printing deals, but today, that very same publication can be achieved by just a push of a button. Businesses which were hard to do before are much easier to do today. What needed you to be fully resourced with millions and billions of dollars on top of heavy networks to undertake can now be achieved with just the simplest computer you can ever find. Getting your business to grow even across boarder needed you to have millions and billions of dollars and so much more, today you can do business around the world while you are still in your house behind your computer.

In today's world which we live in, this is not a myth or fiction, we have so many success stories, true stories that we can attest to. Stories which can prove beyond reasonable doubt that you don't have to be big to start, you just have to start to become big. Stories that proves that you don't have to have much to be successful, anything that you have in your hand can bring out everything you have ever imagined to achieve. Stories that proves that you don't have to be old and experienced to achieve much, you just have to rise to the occasion to pursue what your mind perceives to be possible and pursue it no matter the circumstances until the day of its manifestation comes. *Bitcoin* is the world's biggest bank with no actual cash. *Uber* is the largest taxi company, but it owns no vehicles. *Facebook* is the world's most popular media owner but it creates no content. *Alibaba* is the most valuable retailer but it has no inventory. *Airbnb* is the world's largest accommodation provider but it owns no real estate. Who would have thought that this is possible?

You will always remain mediocre with the crowd until you are willing to go a little further by yourself. Never use another person as your standard, you have to always measure yourself against who you are inside, against the purpose which has been given to you by God. These other companies that are celebrated worldwide may have done great exploits to date, but I believe without a shadow of doubt that that's not the best that can ever be done on this planet earth. The Bible records that *"no eye has seen nor ear has heard, neither has it entered the heart of man what the Lord has in store for them that loves him"*, hear me, it doesn't matter who you are or where you come from, you are exactly where the market needs you to do great exploits. Who thought that a car can move without fuel? Elon Musk dared to pursue the success of this great vision. Who ever thought that the world could interact and stay in touch at a social level in one platform at any time despite of their geographic location? Mark Zuckerberg and other guys believed this to be possible and pursued the dream to see it becoming a reality that we all benefit from.

But here is the thing, you don't get to achieve the level of these entrepreneurs' success by just wishing to be as successful as they are. Business is more than just the development of its craft, but a complete understanding of how to manage the business of the craft developed. In my country alone, more than 85% of companies die every single year. More than 60% of these companies were funded by government programs and private banks. You can imagine the rate of abortion of potential sustainable jobs that occurs concurrently with this kind of incidences across the country. Look, the statistics may not be as accurate as they should be, but this fact may not debunk nor discredit the fact that there are thousands or even millions of entrepreneurs out there struggling. The sad truth is that these struggles that entrepreneurs go through can all be traced back to ignorance. Most entrepreneurs don't know what they are doing. Entrepreneurship is a knowledge based entity. There is a set of knowledge, paradigm system and principles that you need to arm yourself with to build your business success.

It is my belief, no matter how controversial it may sound, that if there was any entrepreneur that was to succeed and be globally celebrated and even be globally impactful in our day and age was the entrepreneur that was to think like an entrepreneur and act like a prostitute.

CHAPTER 1

INTRODUCTION

"How we think shows through in how we act. Attitudes are mirrors of the mind. They reflect thinking"

- David Joseph Schwartz

The world is changing every single day. In business, it is becoming more evident every day that business is not as usual as we were made to believe. Change. There is literally nowhere we can hide from it in this fast-paced world. Our ability to navigate through this change as entrepreneurs in today's era will be one of our (if not the only) greatest assets in creating a better future for our businesses. The people's needs are changing every single day as we get to learn more about our impact in the environment, and as a result, we tend to see many different changes that happens in the market trends. Some of which has swallowed up many big and small corporations in the process. The world as we know it has been divided into three major markets; mature markets, emerging markets and less affluent markets. These are the markets that as we intend to journey with entrepreneurship, we are setting ourselves to serve.

Entrepreneurship is about solving problems. It is about improving the quality of lives of people living around us and those living in countries we may never personally set foot in. Many governments are facing different challenges in their efforts to provide a lucrative business environment for their entrepreneurs, from stabilizing inflations with interest rates adjustments in this era where economies are slowing down while inflation is hiking up. Technology has also played a very huge role in changing how we live life today. Our needs has changed and so is our wants. This has not only changed how we live life today, but it has also changed how business should be done. Business is no longer more concerned about what you sell, but how you sell it.

Although the needs of the people vary for each market, there are major drivers for consumption at each touch point that affects how consumers interact with the world. In the end, all these needs are the drivers of the trends and growing businesses such as yours. In other words, the future of your business lies within your ability to surf the waves of these trends. Finding balance, building momentum and moving forward. This is why it is paramount for you as an entrepreneur to see how you can position yourself and your business to remain relevant in the market.

It is so easy to discredit this book just by reading the tittle. Of course, to some it is very captivating. I'm one of the people who are so excited about this topic. We have no problem with thinking like an entrepreneur, in fact, I think by now we see the need for us to think like entrepreneurs, it is what we really want and love to do. But wait, act like a prostitute? Most of us have never imagined these two extremes seating next to each other in a black and yellow taxi. It is an exciting yet potentially controversial topic. I remember the facial expressions I always saw on people's faces when I told them that I'm writing this book. Look, I get it, okay? There's so much we know about prostitutes, mostly the things that we feel that they are bad for our liking. There's also so much we don't know, or so much we don't want to know about prostitution. There's so much that entrepreneurs can learn from prostitutes. What if I told you that this is possibly the only thing standing between you and your wildest success in business?

You made a very wise choice to buy this book. For sure, what you may not be aware of is the fact that by buying this book you were not only investing on your own growth as an entrepreneur, but you were also investing in a vision that is seeking to revolutionalize entrepreneurship and raise globally competitive entrepreneurs out of Africa. If you are an entrepreneur or a business person, this book is for you. If you feel inside of you that your local market and your country is just too small for your vision, you need a bigger market to affect, this book is for you. If you want to be a globally competitive entrepreneur, this book is also for you. If you are saying that you are clueless about entrepreneurship or running a business, this is your book too. If you are saying *"I have a business (or I've been in business) but I don't know why my business is not performing the way I wanted"*, this is your book too. Look, if you are sick and tired of being a small entrepreneur, let me be the one to tell you that your days of smallness are over.

By the time you will reach the last page of this book, things should be starting to take shape in your business. It doesn't matter which part of the world you are reading this book from, your business will never be the same again. I must emphasize the words of my mentor, *Boago F Ramogapi*, which he likes to repeatedly remind me that, *"it is not about what you hear that matters, but what you do with what you hear that matters the most"*. Let this book not be just one of those great books you have ever read, let it be the book that provoked you to rise up to do something about your dream with a better understanding, revelation and inspiration. Are you not tired of the frustrations of being small outside yet you know that you are big inside? I told myself that this may be my first book to be published, but since it's written by me, it better be so good that it gets the attention of the world. We serve a global God, why should we be local?

In my experience of coaching a few startups that I was coaching at Launchit Coaching International, I've got to realize that a lot of people who decides to start businesses have no basic understanding of few vital things. I've got to meet a lot of people whose interest was to just get into the business and the rest they will figure it out later. The moment they start the business everything begins to crumble down and their only comment is that *"I have no idea what's going on"*. Statistics reports were released in Botswana in the year 2013 that revealed that at least 85% of businesses die every single year in Botswana. Most of which are start-ups. I believe that this very same statistics could be true even in your country. The numbers may not be as accurate as they should be, but this cannot discount nor discredit the fact that there are hundreds, thousands and even millions of entrepreneurs out there struggling. And you could be one of them. Entrepreneurs, more especially start-ups face countless of challenges that ultimately kill their dreams that they were looking forward towards celebrating as their successes.

In Africa, we have many starters and very few finishers. It is not about how many businesses start-up in Africa, it is about how many of them actually grow and expand even to other markets. Look, I have been to a business school for three years. I have been hands on in running a business, both mine and other people's. I know that's not much of experience for some, but if you give me a few minutes, please allow me to share with you few words of wisdom that I've learnt in this side of the world, and that which I've got to know through the inspiration from God about ***entrepreneurship***.

CHAPTER 2

THE POWER OF SMALL THINGS

"While it may seem small, the ripple effects of small things is extraordinary"

- Matt Bevin

Craig Groeschel once said that *"it is often the small things that no one sees that result in the big things that everyone wants"*. One of the things that most of entrepreneurs fail to understand is the great power of small things. We want to be big, which is good, but we think it takes doing big things to be big. Sometimes we also think that it takes big challenges to kill gigantic businesses. But guess what? It is all in the small things. A simple decision can take the whole company's future down the drain. We have heard about this things before, for example, Kodak's refusal to embrace digital photography or even Blockbuster's demise after turning down a chance to purchase Netflix in the emerging era of video-on-demand. Both the successes and failures of businesses around the world can be traced back to the small things that they did (or didn't do) that made the big difference that we see today. Right now we are yet to witness another great history being made between the two rivalries of all times, McDonalds and a new company founded by former executives of McDonalds, Shake Shack. Talk about disruption.

Excellence is the result of the full attention paid to each detail of the whole component. For those of you who are already running businesses, you need to take time and introspect, ask yourself questions. Be honest with yourself, ask yourself this question; *" what is it that I'm doing (or not doing) today that will kill my business tomorrow?"* The truth is, a lot of us know the answer to the above question, but we still find ourselves seemingly ignoring these things that doesn't only threaten the health of our businesses but its life and destiny. There are many entrepreneurs out there today who still wish in regret that if only they had attended to these small things sooner than they did, they would have been far right now in their entrepreneurship journey. I know that we love learning from mistakes, but sometimes it doesn't have to be your own mistake for you to learn from it, some mistakes are unnecessary and can be avoided.

Just like raising a baby from birth, growing a business needs special attention. Not just attention, but a specific form of attention to specific things in the business. A lot of us as African entrepreneurs, we are too lazy to look closely to these things. The truth is, we fail in business not because of poor quality ideas, but we fail simply because of poor management. We are lazy to think. Look, we all get ideas every now and then on how we can best improve our businesses, or rather what businesses to start. But guess what? We never even bother to implement those. We take a lot of things casual, even when we see it will bring demise in the future.

It is very important for us as African entrepreneurs to understand that in every goal that we set ourselves to achieve, things never end wrong, things always start wrong. Failure is a result of something both done and undone. Happiness or sadness is also a result of things done and undone. I remember a quote I once read on Twitter that says *"proper prior preparation prevents poor pathetic performance"*. Ladies and gentlemen, it is of great importance (if not a necessity) for us to understand that foreknowledge of the enemy and his tactics is key in the preparation for the battle that's ahead. The Bible (for those who've had the privilege to read it) records in Proverbs 4:7 that;

"Wisdom is supreme. Get wisdom. Yes, though it costs all your possessions, get understanding."

Most of us we just dive into the business world without knowing at least a few basic things about running a business. I'm not saying that it is wrong, you don't have to wait to know everything for you to start, but it will take your knowledge to stay in business for the longest time. Either way, you still have to learn. I'm fully aware that most of us have not been fortunate enough to enroll with institutes of higher learning for a few courses on proper business management. We thank God for giving us the opportunity to be holding this book in our own hands. Your knowledge is about to upgrade to that of a sharp entrepreneur.

There are so many small things that killed a lot of businesses both big and small. Under normal circumstances, you would expect a huge giant to be killed by a gigantic enemy. But that's not always the case. Just like Goliath was killed by David in the Bible, such is the case with many different companies around the world. Similarly, it is the small things that contributed to the successes of many businesses around the world. We said this in the previous chapter that in today's business world, it is not about what you are selling but how you are selling it. The magic is not in starting a business, the magic is in staying in business. You stay in business if you are able to continually stay relevant to meet the needs of the people.

Here is one of the small things that will take your business far; understand future trends, keep healthy relationships with your partners and clients, stay relevant, manage your money well, and always keep a smile on a customer's face. When you serve a client, the idea is not to transact in that current transaction, the idea is to transact from that same person in the future. A friend of mine, Wazer, went to the United States for the first time in 2016, when he got there he went to this other cell phone dealer in the shopping center next to where he was staying. As he was browsing through a wide range of cellphones that were displayed there, a certain gentleman who works there in the store walked to him to check if he needs help. He didn't know it was the manager. He asked him, *"What's your name Sir?"* Wazer told him the name. He took him through the aisles and showing him some of the hot deals that they had in store at the time. After buying a cell phone in the store, the manager offered him a free screen protector. As though that was not enough, when Wazer went back to the United States again after six full months, he went to that same store to buy a USB cord (because he fell in love with the customer service at the store), as he was walking in the store the manager came by and shouted, *"Hey Wazer, it's been a long time man, how have you been"*. He called him by his name. Wazer was shocked.

That's what customers loves. Personalization. They want to do business with people that they can trust. It is more than what you are doing for them but how you make them feel about serving them. Relationships. That's the backbone of the future of your business. I can tell you this, he hasn't told me yet, but I believe Wazer will never buy his gadgets anywhere else in the United States except from that store. That's what you want as an entrepreneur, to be sure of future business from your clients. Not because you have contracts that binds your customers to keep buying from you, but because you have a working relationship that benefits the both of you. The power of small things.

Now imagine, what really got to me is that this store attracts hundreds of people from all the corners of the United States, and each of their customer feels the same way as Wazer does about the store. They feel home. Did they spend money to keep Wazer? No, they didn't. Just a smile, free gifts, and of course, remembering his name. Now he is glued forever. What's funny now is that I'm already a fan of that store even though I have never been there personally, and guess what, the day God opens a door for me to go to the United States, I want to go to that that store and be one of the clients of that store.

Customers talk. They recommend. This is why they say *"branding is not about what you tell people about yourself, it is about what people tell others about you"*. There is power in the small things, enough power to make you a very successful entrepreneur.

CHAPTER 3

ARE ENTREPRENEURS BORN OR MADE?

Just like with leaders, there are a lot of debates going on around the world with a lot of people seeking to come to the conclusion about the origin of entrepreneurs. Are entrepreneurs born or made? Well, my submission here is rather primarily premised on my personal opinion with regards to this topic. Before we dive straight into it, we have to first establish that there are people who feel like entrepreneurship is not for them. Which is understandable. But within the same group of people there are those who don't consider themselves potential candidates for entrepreneurship simply because within their mental faculties they think that entrepreneurship has its own people who are born for it. Just like in leadership, there are still a lot of people out there who holds the opinion that leaders are born and not made. To me entrepreneurship is some kind of a calling.

If you look at all the entrepreneurs that we celebrate today, there is something about how passionate they are about what they are doing. Given how tough it is out there in this journey (although a lot of people have made it to seem so glamorous and easy), they still press on with great tenacity and enthusiasm. There is just *"that thing"* about them. The *oomph*! Entrepreneurship is about solving problems. The statement itself sounds so easy, but the reality of the realization of this statement is so cruel and probably the hardest thing in life. I believe entrepreneurs are not born. I also believe that they are not made. Entrepreneurs are born to be made. Anyone can be an entrepreneur even though not everyone will be an entrepreneur. Life has a way of channeling us through circumstances that will develop certain infuriation and desires pertaining to what will ultimately become what we are passionate about, not just passionate, but passionate towards righting that wrong.

It is through this process that we end up having people concluding what their purposes for their lives are. All done with the same objective of creating a better world for our future generations. It is through this process that we end up having those that life has channeled their lives through paths that developed the passion in them to develop solutions that later gets commercialized and consequently generate profits for the growth and sustenance of that solution. I have said this before that I'm not an entrepreneur because I have always been passionate about entrepreneurship, I became an entrepreneur because life has made me one. I believe God has a purpose for my life. I believe that's why he allowed me to be ***born*** in the family that I was born in with the condition that it had which ***made*** me the entrepreneur that I am today. It now makes sense to me why I was born with the skills, abilities and the knowledge that I was born with. They are my greatest assets in achieving this which I believe without a shadow of a doubt that it is my purpose on earth. We all go through what we go through for us to become what we have to become.

CHAPTER 4

DREAM BIG

"If you have a dream that you can achieve by yourself, it is not worth it. Your dream should be bigger than you."

- Bishop TD Jakes

I felt extremely blessed to have been there in that historic moment led by my mentor, Coach BF Rams, the history maker, the uncommon man, as he brought Bishop TD Jakes for the very first time in the history of history in Botswana. I was so excited, but I couldn't believe that it is actually happening, and that I'm right there in the same room seated in the same VVIP aisle with Bishop TD Jakes, like the real Bishop TD Jakes from Dallas Texas in the United States of America. The world's top preacher, entrepreneur and movie producer. What I have been seeing on YouTube and many other short video clips, I could now see with my own eyes. It was a dream that I never thought its realization could be that easily possible.

I love what Coach said when he opened the meeting with a few remarks, he said, *"there is no place where you want to go to in life where no one has been before"*. Most of the things that we want to achieve in life has already been achieved by other people before. But the problem is that we always feel like we can't achieve those things because they seem bigger than us. We feel too small to achieve such kind of successes. Some of us feel undeserving to achieve those dreams, we feel like those big dreams can only be achieved by other people and not us. I say this all the time that most people believe that it is possible for anyone to be a Billionaire, but they have a tough time believing that the same Billionaire can be them.

If you are to dream, go all out. Dream big. Dream crazy. Look, this is not your first time to hear these words, and it is probably not the last time. You need to look at yourself as a global player. You need to look at yourself as a nation. You need to look at yourself as an international standard business enterprise. For as long as your planning, your dreaming and your conduct as an entrepreneur is locally oriented, mediocrity will never lack in what you do. See people in different countries around the world using your product or service. See your products or services making headlines in languages you cannot understand. You have been consuming products and services of other entrepreneurs around the world for so long now that you have made them part of your life, your life is almost nonexistent without them. But you want to be comfortable with a few customers from your neighborhood consuming your products or services occasionally.

You are bigger than your community. You are bigger than your city. You are even bigger than your country. You are bigger than your continent. You have been created by a global God for a global impact. Don't limit yourself to your surroundings. Don't limit yourself to your language. Your country is a good launch pad for your business, that's why you have to start in your country with all the help you can get, but never lose the sight of your vision that you are building a global business.

Never underestimate the power of the "small idea" that you have. Don't look down upon what your brain has produced. God has made in us different people with different forms of intelligence. But this is what I can tell you, we may be different but we were all made for one thing; to make a difference, and we can all make a difference somewhere in someone's life just by what our minds conceives. Your community may not accept or even see value in what you do, but I will tell you this, there are thousands and even millions of people outside your community who are dying to benefit from what you are doing. You have to see a way of reaching out to those people. You may not have the capacity to do it all by yourself, and that's how it should feel like, because that's the way it should feel like.

If your dream can be achieved all by yourself, it is too small to make a global footprint. At least within the business sphere. You need to know that your business will never grow beyond you, and if you are to build your business in the foundation of your individual capacity to deliver, your business will never be bigger than you. For you to build something bigger than you, bigger than your community, bigger than your country, you have to dream big. Think disruption. Think global. Set yourself for the global market. Set yourself to survive the fiercely competitive global markets in this dog-eat-dog world. You can do it. Strive Masiyiwa is an example, an African like you from a village unknown to the world, but made up his mind to be a globally competitive entrepreneur and he indeed became one, going after big bloated corporations and challenged them to a bigger fight that he is fighting very well and winning.

Dream big. Dream for the future. Think a hundred years from now. How will the world be like? How will your industry be like? Ten years ago Forbes magazine put up a headline in its front page saying, *"Nokia, one billion customers - can anyone catch the cellphone king?"* As we speak now, ten years later, we all know who the cellphone king is. This is what you need to see, many of these businesses that are worth billions of dollars today didn't even exist a few years ago. The world is changing every day. Your business could be relevant now, but how will it be relevant tomorrow.

Do you even know where the world is going? Have you ever heard about *'the internet of things'?* Do you see how technology is changing the world? Do you see how technology is shaping the future of our business world? You may not be interested in being a global business player, no problem, but you should start opening your eyes to see what's going on around you. In today's world, even if you don't go to the world, the world is coming to you. In fact, the world is already there with you. When you look at your local shopping malls and your city's CBD, what do you see? Do you see your country, or do you see the world? We are already part of the global business world. And here is the thing, you cannot afford to be a part of a game you don't understand.

You may have read before about companies in the developed world buying each other out, the time for such to happen in this African continent has come. I have to say this, I have no problem with companies buying each other, and my worry is, who will be buying who? Will the African companies be buying each other out? Or will the companies from other continents buying the African companies out. Dream big. Think tomorrow. We will never beat technology. Technology has made it possible for many businesses to start. Technology has made it possible for other businesses to grow faster. Technology has made it possible for other businesses to expand faster. You can be in a village somewhere and build something that will be worth billions in a few years to come, because of technology.

Take time to learn about where the world is going. Be part of the conversations around the world which talks about the direction which the world is taking, more especially the conversations that talks about bringing changes to how we will be doing our day to day businesses. Leaders of innovation around the world are already talking. They are strategizing about how to bring a complete change to our business activities to ease trade and our day to day operations. You need to know what they are talking about. Don't be left behind. This will affect your business one way or the other in a few years to come.

Business leaders around the world today are talking about artificial intelligence. They are talking about fintech (finance & technology). They are talking about data science. They are talking about disruption. They are talking about innovation, analytics, retail, wearables, entrepreneurship and technology. They are talking about blockchain. They are talking about machine learning and customer experience. They are talking about healthcare and design thinking. These may sound like big terms, but hidden within these terms is a knowledge you need to have. In today's business world, you will only survive because you know stuff and you plan ahead. You will only survive because you dream big, bigger than what you see today with your own eyes. You will survive because you have given yourself to pursuing something that's bigger than you. Something that will need other people to be on board with their resources for it to be possible. Something that will continue to make impact even years after you have long departed from earth.

You were created by a global God, think big, and think global. Pursue global impact. You can do it. Think like an entrepreneur. Always keep this in mind, in today's world, you can be coming from one of most poorest of the poorest families in one of the smallest villages in the world and still build a business, a product or a service that will shake the world and completely change your life and the lives of those around you for generations. Could it be possible that you holding this book marks the beginning of the greatest things that are about to happen by you, through you and with you? Dream big.

CHAPTER 5

BEWARE OF 'ACHIEVEMENTS'

"Sometimes the good is the enemy of the best"

- Mogotsi D. Baloyi

Never be content with where you are, there's always another higher dimension to reach. Most of the people today are not killed by their failures, they are killed by their successes. No enemy relaxes after being defeated, they will always want to retaliate. They will want to retreat and regroup to attack back. And most of us, when the enemy attacks back, he finds us relaxed, unarmed and swimming in the pool of our past successes. When I grew up, I always wondered. There was this certain old man, my mom had told me about his multiple business successes. He always passed by our house with his then big car to one of his shops. Almost every day. This is what shocked me, I asked myself, if this man has the amount of money that he is alleged to have, why is he still waking up every morning to pursue more money?

Imagine, say you were to wake up in the morning to a bank balance of about a hundred million US dollars, that's like *one billion pulas,* what would you do? Most of us will go on emergency leave the whole of the following week, some of us might consider closing the business for good. It may not be you, but you will be surprised how many of us are so not used to certain levels of achievement that when we achieve ten times more than we have anticipated, we feel like we have arrived and therefore there is no need for us to pursue the journey further. Have you wondered why Bill Gates still wakes up every morning to spend about 15% of his time to brainstorm with his teams at Microsoft? With all the worth that he has amassed in his entrepreneurial journey, he is still disciplined to continue pursuing higher dimensions of his entrepreneurial ambitions.

The problem with most of us is that when we create businesses we create them to feed our stomach and not building legacies. We are creating them for our survival. We are doing what the Zimbabweans call *"hunt-*

ing with the salt in the pocket". We enter the bush ready to eat (with immediate effect) whatever we kill. Look, most of us we were moved by hunger into the battlefield of entrepreneurship, myself included. When I say hunger I don't only mean hunger for success, I mean hunger, literally. No food in the stomach, and not only in the stomach but also in the house. It got worse during one of the days when this happened and my mom sent me to borrow a few kilograms of maize meal and I realized that not only our family was hungry but the rest of our street was hungry too. Literally. Well, of course except for the rich big housed families that we couldn't just knock their doors anyhow.

Having grew up like this, most of what we do has been designed to move profits from hand to the mouth all the time. It is a habit that got imprinted in our psychology over time. Life never gave us the opportunity to look at profits as seeds for sowing and not bread for eating. We were never taught how to build wealth for generations to come. I have asked this before and I will ask it again, pardon my English, but, apart from your surname, what else has your grandfather left for you? Where is the business or businesses that they were running? You need to understand that we are the generation that has been created to do business better than before in Africa.

We are the generation that is standing a very good space to pioneer businesses that will reach more a hundred years to come. We are the generation that has been created to create globally competitive businesses that will add value to the people of the world for generations to come. We are who Africa has been waiting for. You are the one your country has been waiting for. A new breed of entrepreneurs is rising in Africa. A breed which will not be satisfied with serving their locally community only. A breed which will create businesses that will serve products consumed by Asians, the Americans, Africans and the rest of the people around the world. This is the breed of entrepreneurs that is taking Africa by a storm.

If you were to continue doing business the way you are doing it right now, both you and them that will start businesses today, in hundred years, their businesses will be multinational corporations and maybe yours will have long died if not the same as it was lots of years back. Build for growth. Build for generations. When you get money, invest in building your legacy rather than spending it on building a lifestyle.

When your goal is to build for lifestyle it will reflect on your financial decisions and aspirations, and you're your goal is to build for legacy it will also reflect on your financial decisions and aspirations.

If you got into business for lifestyle, when you make the money you start feeding your lifestyle cravings. Your ego. You will want to buy the big cars first, wear expensive clothes and watches, and be seen on long expensive vacations, swipe expensive wines for friends and strangers. You live for the now. But while you do that, there are men and women out there building empires. There are men and women out there erecting major passive income streams that will feed them and their children's children for years. They are building for tomorrow and beyond. When they die, they don't leave their children with debts and surnames, they live them with empires. And not just empires, empires they built for over twenty years. They don't just leave them with the empires, they leave them with empires they trained them over the years to run.

They don't settle for small achievements, they go for the bigger fish in the pond. They expand their territories. They keep tapping into untapped markets and dimensions. The Bible says *"a good man leaves an inheritance even for the third generation"*. Look at your business, imagine your grandchild seating on that chair as the great competent Chief Executive Officer in your business. Don't relax because you have made a few good strides in your business. In fact, congratulations, you have just gained a new responsibility to fight harder. Nobody relaxes after being defeated. They will keep wanting to bounce back. Whatever you fight to get, you will have to fight to keep.

Do yourself a favor, learn to celebrate progress. It is very important to appreciate yourself when you have done well. I've had many of those moments of pausing, reflecting and giving myself adequate appreciation for what I have achieved this far. But this is the thing, I have got to learn that no matter how big your achievements are, never relax on yesterday's victories. Nelson Mandela once said *"After climbing a great hill, one only finds that there are many more hills to climb"*. No matter how great your achievements are, your better days are not behind you, your better days are ahead of you.

There are more hills climb. There are more markets to launch into. There are more products to launch. There are more books to right. This could be the only book you read this month, did you know that there are people who reads 15 books a month? Yes, there is always a higher dimension to ascend to. Keep pushing yourself. The more you win, the more you should refine your strategies. Every single year, review how you will do business differently in the following year. Let your hunger for more grow. It is not greed, it is calling pushing limits. Social media people will call it 'levels'. They have no limits.

CHAPTER 6

YOU ARE EXACTLY WHERE THE MARKET NEEDS YOU

"From the smallest families of the smallest villages often comes the greatest of the greatest."

-Unknown

Vusi Thembekwayo once said *"you might be having a disadvantaged background, but you don't have a disadvantaged brain"*. I think that explains why we as African entrepreneurs needs to understand as he explained that where we come from is actually part of our strength and not our disadvantage. Look, I'm not trying to motivate you. In fact, I wouldn't even bother. You've heard this words more than a million times before. You have probably said the same words to countless people before. It is easy to believe them when said to the other person than when it is said to you. A lot of us entrepreneurs sometimes we get tired of attending these 'motivational seminars' and listening to motivational speakers. We wish we could just attend a seminar which will bring actual monetary turnaround in our businesses. We are used to telling people what to do and that is why a lot of us have a problem with being told what to do.

It is easy to take for granted what we repeatedly hear or say. It doesn't matter who you are or where you come from, you are existing in your condition for a reason. If we are to talk about success then we must deal with your condition which is building you up for that success. Entrepreneurship is about solving problems. That is why it has been said a couple of times that 'there is a very fine line that delineates the difference between an entrepreneur and a businessman'. I will understand if you were to raise your eyebrows by now in shock upon hearing this. To put it in simpler terms of definition; entrepreneurs analyze their environment to look for problems to solve through tapping into their creativity and innovation to create solutions which later gets commercialized and consequently generate profits while the businessman looks for what makes money and pursue it.

Of course, I'm fully aware that this is subject to debate based of people's different views of the subject. For example, there are millions of businessmen who deem themselves as entrepreneurs and it dents their image when we put our definition of the two as aforementioned. I will give you a simple example, say there are two guys, Brian and Benjamin, Brian out of common concern of high temperature rise due to the growing effects of global warming in his location decides to professionally package branded ice-pops of a certain quality and taste. He then rolls out his product in the market. As it grows into the market, becoming popular, Benjamin begins to see that ice-pops are making a lot of money. Then he decides to buy ice-pops from Brian and sell them in his area with markup.

Now tell me, between Brian and Benjamin, who is an entrepreneur and who is a businessman? Now, of course these two people will be deemed by the world as entrepreneurs. An entrepreneur meaning an individual who owns or runs an enterprise, according to the definition of the majority. I used to think like that too before. I am not forcing you to take my definition of these two. In fact, hear me twice, I am not in any way saying that there is anything wrong with being a businessman.

We must understand that we exist in a world which is what it is because of the different ecosystems that has been growing over the time. Ecosystems will teach us that we cannot all be the same, because then there will be no balance in the society which is very imperative to uphold a growing economy and the quality of life in general. It is the same as what I dealt with during one of my Facebook Live videos which I do as often as I can, the silent debate that's in the mouths of the many about the superiority of entrepreneurs over employees. Another topic for another day. In fact, let me just throw in a few things at you regarding this topic. There is nothing wrong with wanting to commit yourself to be an employee.

Of course we exist in an era in the world where entrepreneurship development has been making all the headlines and for the longest period of time many people have been feeling guilty for not seeing possibilities of them becoming an entrepreneur. We are not all entrepreneurs. We can't all be entrepreneurs. God made in us different people. Invested in us all are different ideas, abilities and skills which God has purposely installed in us for his divine purpose.

The entrepreneur trades the business idea while the employee trades the skills. All great entrepreneurs will tell you that minus their employees their business is nothing. Of course it's pretty much obvious that minus the entrepreneur the employee is nothing as well. And of course entrepreneurs can afford to fire employees every now and then to suit their workforce needs. But I have seen a lot of people becoming tremendously frustrated and disappointed because they went into business because the society has defined entrepreneurship as the "it" of the now. And as a result, people who work or chose to work for entrepreneurs out there feel inferior while in my view they are not because they are also playing a critical role in the success of the business.

There are people who will make great CEO(s) in other people's businesses yet bad entrepreneurs if they were to run business ventures of their own. It doesn't make sense but it does happen. Know your space and shine in it. Similarly, in the business world we have entrepreneurs and businessmen/businesswomen. These are both business people. There is nothing wrong with Benjamin choosing to see an opportunity to sell Brian's ice-pops and not create his own. At least for the start. Of course we all want to own our own brand at some point. But most entrepreneurs that's where they make their biggest mistake.

One thing we need to understand is that the business world just like any other ecosystems has different components. And in all these different business processes we as entrepreneurs need to thoroughly definc our part based on ability and passion. There is a song that I love so much, it's called 'glorious', I met the song on Facebook one time when I was not feeling very well about myself, the song was sang by very little kids, one of the words that I loved from the lyrics of the song were the words that said *"it's like a symphony, just keep listening, and pretty soon you will start to figure out your part. Everyone plays a piece, and there are melodies, each one of us"*. It taught me about the diversity of things, as an entrepreneur, I began to relate it to entrepreneurship.

It taught me that the most important thing is to understand that the business world is like a symphony, I just have to keep on carefully and slowly analyzing it, pretty soon I will figure out my part. This was the time when I was asking myself questions about the future of my company because I couldn't seem to be getting the picture of how we can best position ourselves in the market. Of course the whole consultancy industry is a very broad industry. It required one to know his/her area of interest as well as capability. Otherwise you will find yourself running after what other consultants do and it works for them and yet it doesn't work for you. Every business person needs to identify their area of operation.

The business world is a huge pie, we can all have our slice from it. Of course our greed will continually lure us towards running after everything while achieving nothing. It is the same with many aspiring entrepreneurs, most of them can't start because they are caught up between thousands of ideas which they equally love. As I said earlier, we need each other as entrepreneurs. A manufacturer needs a distributor, a retailer needs a supplier, and all these guys needs a market-maker. They needs accountants. They needs branding experts. They need legal advisors. They need secretarial services. In what you do as an entrepreneur there is always an opportunity for another entrepreneur to benefit from in your business.

There is what I call *'corporate trade model'* (CTM), which simply means; in what I am doing as an entrepreneur, what business opportunities am I creating for the other entrepreneurs around me? In today's world that's what we need. That's what can practically aid entrepreneurs to work together in serving the communities. Sometimes we don't even need to compete with one another, we have a choice; either to run after the same cake and the best (in whatever way) gets their share of the cake, sometimes the whole cake, or, we all work together as entrepreneurs to bake that cake with different contributions from each of us and then we all get our shares from the cake based on what each entrepreneur contributed. That's the only way entrepreneurship can help millions of African entrepreneurs to start, grow and expand their businesses. That's how we can end up having globally competitive African brands, born and bred on this continent of Africa. *Amandla!* It's called *co-opetition.*

Sometimes you just have to collaborate with your competitors on certain projects. Have you been to a hotel before? Most of you have. Now let me show you this, a hotel is a very nice place to be. All things you need for your relaxation in one place. It's a place that can take you into some refreshing world where you even forget all your stresses. Of course, a good and convenient place for our subject person to make a lot of money from. Location my friend, location. For some of those who have not yet been to a hotel, let me take you through a quick tour of what happens there. Well, I am not saying I am an expert because up to now I can count how many times I have been to a hotel. It's not more than a hundred times. It is well, Jesus is Lord. Anyway, when you get to a hotel, of course they differ according to their star rating.

When you get to a five star hotel, you will have to go to the reception to make a booking and check-in. If you look around the reception you going to see a very well decorated lounge with some television screen, magazines, Wi-Fi (Hallelujah), juice and so many other different things. All free, Amen? Before you know it, they will give you a key to your room and some guy will arrive with a trolley and load your luggage and guide you to your room. On the corridors you will walk past well-crafted designs mounted on the wall. You could pick a very welcoming and refreshing breeze coming from all ends of the hotel. When you get to your room, you are going to find a very arranged room, very comfortable bed, clean towels in the shower, toiletry as well, television screen with DSTV (it depends), a desk, a telephone, cremoras and other tea ingredients, and so many glorious things.

Once you are settled in, after a short while your phone will ring, when you pick it up you will hear an anointed voice saying *"Good evening Sir, it is reception, dinner is ready"*. You go to the restaurant, there is free Wi-Fi all over. There is a bar as well. I believe you can walk past a gym on your way there. When you get there you will meet another amazing group of people smiling at you and guiding you to your table. When you go to the buffet, variety my friend, variety. You can eat all you want, as many as you want. Even desserts. Don't worry about getting stomach pains, there is a massage spa somewhere within the hotel. You want to run around town? There are cabs just right outside. It's a glorious place to be at.

But this is what many people don't see, behind all these simplified and glorious experiences, there are tens and thousands of entrepreneurs who are working hard together behind the scenes to render either a service or product that makes up the entire hotel experience. Of course you paid once at the reception, but when you did, you were paying all these entrepreneurs for the contribution they made. They baked your cake together, and when you paid your invoice, each got their share equivalent to their contribution as per their contract. That's what we need as entrepreneurs. To join hands and form industries. To form ecosystems. Our problem is that we like working alone thinking that we will make it, sponsored by our greed. We need to form corporate trade models that will nurture and grow our businesses.

There is a huge pie out there for all of us. I normally ask this question; how much is all the money in the whole world? There is a huge cake out there in the business world, it's like a symphony, you just have to keep listening, and pretty soon you will start to figure out your part. You can't do everything. Your greedy heart will tell you that you can, your wiser self will show you that you can't. I used to think I can too, it's a stage everyone will get the opportunity to go through. Find your part in the industry, start something, grow it and expand. Go out there and prostitute it to as many people as you possibly can. We don't make money out of the number of people we can count in the market, we make money out of the number of transactions we register in our businesses.

I was given the opportunity to share the stage with Botswana's first youngest female Member of Parliament, Honorable Bogolo Kwenewendo at a university event in Botswana titled *The Business Intervention*, amongst the panel there was other amazing young people from Botswana and Lesotho as well. Hon Kwenewendo made a very remarkable statement during her elucidation as she was giving the keynote address, she said, *"Many of us we are losing out on business opportunities because we think they are not western enough"*. I said *"My God, that's the problem right there"*. I got reminded of the times when I really wished I was born in China. Well, I was right, I could be Jack Ma by now. But what we fail to understand is that God created us as solutions to the communities that we exist in. It is not a mistake that you were born in the family that you were born in.

Of course, you didn't choose your parents, you didn't choose your face, you didn't choose your home village, you didn't choose the colour of your skin, and you didn't choose how you are. You also didn't choose your abilities, your skills, and your passions. You didn't choose anything. You just found yourself the way you are. Trust me, you are at the right place at the right time. You might be relevant to the time in terms of existence, but you will only be relevant to your location the day you begin to act on your ideas, skills and abilities. The truth is that we fail to be content in what God has given us. Just because the idea held by the next entrepreneur sounds a bit sophisticated than ours means that ours is worth less or even worthless. We want to be like other people. We want to make the monies others make by doing what they do. What we don't know is that they made money out of staying true to who they are and what God gave them to trade. I posted on Facebook one time and I said *"money is money"*. It doesn't matter what you trade, in the end, money is money. Forex money is money, books money is money, hairdos money is money, and tech money is money.

The more we focus on other people, the lesser value we begin to see in ourselves. This is one thing that really draws us back as entrepreneurs. When *Prince Mazibuko* was giving a presentation during the first annual *Pioneers Festival*, he paused and came to stand in front of me, he said to me, *"Goitsemang, you need to believe in yourself more than anyone who believes in you"*. He made another resounding statement, many of you may not be of our faith, but just read, he said, *"if the early church did not believe in Christ, how were they going to sell Christ to us today that we may believe in him?"*. You will get it later. Your customers will not believe in your product/service if you yourself do not believe in it. We have heard this a couple of times before. And you cannot act on something you don't believe in.

Many of us have lost business opportunities simply because we didn't believe in them as much as we should. Until somebody else, most of the time a foreigner, comes to do what you were supposed to do and make millions out of it. I know what I am talking about. You need to understand that your community is counting on you. You need to know that God and Heaven are counting on you. The difference between a seed and a tree is time and experience. It is the impossibilities that provides a platform for miracles. *"Difficulties provokes a miracle, but impossibilities provokes great miracles"*.

We have studied about the likes of Henry Ford who built the first car in the world. This is the man who later said, *"Whether you think you can or cannot, you are right"*. We have studied about the likes of Bill Gates and Steve Jobs. We have our own African icons such as the young man from Cameroon, he calls himself Kelvin Doe AKA DJ Focus. He built a community radio station from scratch using electronic parts he got from a scrap yard somewhere in his community every time he passed there from school. A junior school student, and you are almost fifty years old and letting your gifts die. Or probably still a member of the '*Worriers &*

Complainers Association Worldwide'. And you call yourself an entrepreneur. Entrepreneurs are not part of the problem, they are part of the solution. That's where you need to be.

I tell people all the time, there is a reason why certain complaints comes to your attention and not the next person. There is something in you that is responding to your outside world. There is a solution in you that's responding to the challenges that it is supposed to solve in the outside world. It is meant to be out there doing what it as designed to do, not in your head. Imagine, what would have happened if Steve Jobs and Bill Gates decided to just sit on their idea and do nothing about it? What would have happened if the guys who made the internet possible could have just sat on the idea? What would have happened if your parents decided not to go ahead with the idea of having you? Yes, the world will be doomed. Literally.

Imagine, your life can be on a very serious pause if your cellphone battery die or when the Wi-Fi goes off for some reason. I know a guy who will rather be dead than to be alive with no internet. But imagine, how worse will life be today if these genius guys decided to do what you want to do with your idea? Just sitting on it. If a guy in America could have inconvenienced you here in Africa by just choosing not to implement his idea in America, how much more can you cost the lives of those whom their lives depends on the success of your idea around the world? You might look at yourself and think you are just a boy or girl from a small village in an African country. What you don't see is that you were made by a God who carries a global mandate, everything he does is for the global space. Including creating you as you are right where you are.

It doesn't matter who you are or where you come from, situations and other unpleasant conditions are always going to be on your way. They don't end the day you launch your business, they will continue on coming and going as you grow as an entrepreneur. You are going to encounter many different challenges, some of them will not just sound impossible but also improbable. Real entrepreneurs are wired within themselves with abilities to deal with challenges. They may not know how they are going to tackle them but the desire to conquer will always be there. If you can't stop a war, at least be ready to fight because if you don't you are a dead meat. Why should something that's going to change the lives of millions of people be created and managed with ease?

"As I look over the room today I see young people who will be speaking today with you who are well accomplished in their own rights, and one thing that I can assure you is that these young people just like you were not privileged when they started, but they have made it this far", Lawrence Ookeditse remarked during the *Business Intervention* which I was also invited to speak at. When you seat down to cry about your situation remember that in the same location which you exist in there are other people who are going through the same problem but they are busy prospering day by day in what they want to achieve. It's not about the problem, it's about who you are. How do you look at challenges? How do you look at your condition? Do you see it as a disadvantage or an advantage? Where people see problems entrepreneurs sees opportunities.

Every challenge is a business opportunity. Everything that can be done and people pay you for is a business opportunity. It doesn't matter how small or big it is. It doesn't matter how unsophisticated it sounds. Entrepreneurship is about solving problems not being sophisticated. The simpler the best. If you could learn how to see everything through the lenses of opportunity your life will never be the same again. I am one of the people who realized sooner in life that complaining about things will not solve anything. I used to complain a lot. Whenever I see something wrong I will pull out my phone and go on social media and rant about it. It felt good. I felt responsible. I felt like I am doing something about my problems.

Until one day I attended a seminar which one my mentors, Botswana's former President *Sir Ketumile Masire* made a statement and said, *"you as young people of this generation have a choice to either continue complaining about the problems that we all see around and wait for another generation to come and do something practical about them through offering solutions, or you can get the pleasure of doing that yourselves today and be remembered tomorrow by generations to come like we did"*. It changed my life. He continued to quote the words of America's former president, President John F. Kennedy, *"ask not about what your country can do for you, ask what you can do for your country"*. I said my goodness.

I began to seat down and coach myself on what I should do for my country regarding the same problems which I always complained on social media building likes with. This was the beginning of me. I said to myself, if I had the power, what would I do to solve this challenge of this growing poor academic performance and social ills sweeping away thousands of the destinies and lives of young people in my country and my continent. It took me a while to come to the resolution of what I was going to do. I began to research about the education system, examinations and other related things. I began to investigate each and every stakeholder who according to me were responsible for the overall outcome of the country's general pass rate.

This involved parents, the teachers, the students, the government and the schools including the general community. I went further on to ask myself, if a student was to excel in his examination with my help, what exactly should I be doing to help the student. I said to myself, you know what? We calculate the general pass rate based on the number of students who sat for the examinations and were able to get a certain number of questions in the examination correct. Then I said, that's it right there, that's what I am going to do. I am going to help as many students as possible to get more questions correct in their examination. But now the question was, how am I going to do that because I had two problems? One, I wasn't so smart. Two, there are thousands and thousands of students out there.

Then I said, *"I'm not so smart, but I got an 'A' in design & technology, science and mathematics at junior school. But I don't need those grades anymore"*, this was when I was doing my first year at university. *"I have moved from the bottom 50 in my school out of 206 students to the top 11 in two weeks at some point in my life, this is a testimony that can change someone's life"*. Then I said, how about I group other young people who got better grades at their junior school and high school in other different subjects? I moved around school and recruited them like Jesus was recruiting disciples, I remember I went to a good friend of mine named Kagiso Phije and said to him, *"follow me"*. I said the same to others, about 15 of them, one of them was my cousin, Phenyo Gokatweng who is currently Botswana's youngest professional corporate MC.

That's how I created an NGO called *All Brilliant Minds Organization*, commonly known as *ALBRIMO* in 2011. We went around schools offering free tuition to students, holding different workshops in different schools across Botswana. From that time to date, the organization has managed to get a few schools and one student into the national top. We are talking about schools moving from 25% to 65%, some from 65% to 89.9%. All these through my amazing team made up of graduates and university students from different universities. The organization was declared the 'Best Youth Organization' by the *Human Resource Development Council (HRDC)* in 2017. We are still growing and yet to do even much better in other African countries.

As the time went on, running ALBRIMO built a very good experience in me. I began to learn how to create solutions that will tackle national challenges. Bit by bit. Being faithful in the small things, very big doors began to open up for me to do what I do best, which is creating solutions. I call myself an Idea Engineer. They call me Serial Disruptor, AKA Wizkid. Don't steal my name. Botswana's media houses gave it to me. That's how I now graduated from running ALBRIMO to opening my business coaching firm called *Launchit Coaching International*. We are still solving more complex challenges, it doesn't end, and I chose to be part of the solution always, not the problems. That's what entrepreneurship is about. But the magic is in realizing sooner that you exist in that environment for a reason.

You don't have the solution, you are the solution. You don't have a vision for the world, you are the vision for the world. No wonder the Bible says that *"you are the salt of the earth and the light of the world"*. It's your nature, you can run away from it. You can ignore it but you can't destroy it. That's why even when you will try to get a job somewhere, you just can't fit into the system. You will begin to see opportunities your boss doesn't see. You will try to suggest a few ideas but they won't be taken.

One great pastor, Apostle Mogotsi D. Baloyi, a very wise man, you are missing out if you don't know him, he said something profound during a sermon he was preaching at church, he said, *"what you are going through is not for you but for someone around you"*. Life has a way of making sure that you get firsthand experience of certain life conditions.

The idea is to ignite and arouse an interest in you to rise to the occasion of doing something about challenge. It is upon you to liberate the people who are faced with the same challenge that you have gone through. *"We all go through what we are going through for us to become what we have to become."* I made this statement one time I was given an opportunity to speak at a certain meeting I can't remember. It got me a while to come to this realization. *"All that we go through in life is education that will enable us to be useful to God in the future"*, my pastor said this on the 29th January 2017 at around 12:34hrs during a sermon about the genesis of Moses which he titled *"for future reference"*.

What distinguishes entrepreneurs from the rest of the people is the response they give to a circumstance. Ordinary people complain about the situation but entrepreneurs contemplate about the solution. We become poor and poorer because of the number of the situations we choose to complain about, but we become rich and wealthier because of the problems and challenges we choose to create solutions for. Life has a way of presenting countless opportunities to all of us to become wealthy. It doesn't matter who you are or where you come from. Around the life of every individual there will always be circumstances visible to him/her challenging him/her to do something about it. Life will always challenge your intelligence. Life will always every now and then test the champion you always claim that you are. It has been said many times that those that choose to remain strong and stay longer in the process tend to be the ones whom society will reward in the future.

Many people are worth more than most of us today simply because of the experience they built through allowing themselves to go through what many chose to quit. Entrepreneurship is about solving problems. It starts with solving problems of the societies within which we find ourselves existing in which gave birth to a business idea. It goes down now to solving the problems of the business itself which gives birth to strategies and management skills which will determine our longevity and profitability in business. As an entrepreneur, one day people will ask you, *"How did you make it?"* Ask yourself about the people you always wish you could ask them the same question. What answer are you exactly looking for? Do we see now that entrepreneurship is a knowledge based activity? It is true, failure and success in business can always be traced down to the knowledge resident in the minds of them that make up the leadership of that business. Entrepreneurship requires a certain frameworks of thinking. It needs certain skills set. If at all we are to rise as African entrepreneurs to compete in the global space, we need to attend to the quality of our thinking. Our thoughts, our ideologies and our modus operandi has to reflect that we are interested in generating wealth and creating long lasting legacies which will continue to change lives even long after we are long gone. We will talk in depth about this as the book goes on.

Do you know any one of the many reasons why prostitutes will decide to get into business? Of course, their decision is mostly influenced by their economic situation. But here is what many people don't see; this is an individual dwelling in an environment which is challenged by all unfavorable factors, rather than conforming to the pressures from the challenges around her (like many people would always opt to do), she decides to look for treasures within herself and make up her mind to risk it all to change her economic outlook. Most prostitutes don't even do it for themselves, they do it for their families. To take kids to school. To feed their kids.

I listened to an audio a while back and a great man who never disclosed his identity made a few statements which left me flabbergasted while he was trying to give us a picture of the world today. He said, *"The greatest tragedy in man's life today is not death, it is not unemployment, it is not poverty, but it is conformity"*. We live life today as defined by other people. We live life with the pace set by others. We live our lives with the tone set by others. The pace setters. We are always running after the trends. This is not just something that only exists within the circles of the society but also in most of the entrepreneurs too.

Look, I'm not saying it is wrong to look up to somebody that you get to a point of almost following each every step that they take. It is a good thing, to a certain level. More especially when you are starting off and still trying to find a footing for yourself in the business. But many people have abused this to an extent of brutally damaging their own creativity and innovation. This is why we see what my brother calls *"business mitosis"* around Africa. I don't know about in your country, but in Botswana, if you go around the free markets you will find long queues of about fifteen to twenty tables of people selling the same thing at the same price targeting the same small group of people. Literally. People are lazy to think. Profitability has overtaken value addition. Be inspired by people, but don't turn into them.

"Entrepreneurship is a synonym for liberation because to those that have success with it, it provides them the freedom to be whoever they

want to be. But, more importantly, it provides them with the freedom to uplift others"

- Professor Steven Rogers

CHAPTER 7

THINK LIKE AN ENTREPRENEUR

"The people who shake the world are those who think"

- Mogotsi D. Baloyi

The most common definition of the word 'think' is usually; *'the process of considering or reasoning about something'*. A typical human brain is about 2% of a human body's weight but uses about 20% of its total energy and oxygen intake. As small as the brain is, but you can see how much energy it consumes for it to function the way it does and to impact the body the way it does. Part of the human brain, which is a unique blessing exclusive to human beings only is the ability to think. When I say 'think', I don't mean recalling or just mere thinking whereby you say "I was thinking about getting a new house". That is the first level of thinking, which deals mainly with consideration and reasoning. As human beings, we are gifted differently with different types of intelligences, for example, there are people with spatial intelligence that deals with visualizing the world in 3D, there are those with the naturalist intelligence that deals with understanding living things and reading nature, the people with the logical/mathematical intelligence that deals mainly with quantifying things, making hypothesis and proving them. These are not the only types of human intelligence that are there. The first and most important thing to do for yourself as an entrepreneur is to know the type of intelligence that you carry because it is from that intelligence that you will be able to fully function to the highest levels of your potential to create and add value to the world as you offer relevant solutions to the world.

We live in a fast-paced world that is heavily influenced by technology from all corners of life. The business world is experiencing many changes in the market trends every single month due to continuous adjustments of people's needs around the world. We have said this before that technology has not only changed how we live our lives today but it has also changed how business is done today. We can talk about many examples including Uber seeing how it has completely changed how we use taxis today. The people's needs these days are driven by many factors depending on the type of market that they are based in.

In the three types of markets that we quickly ran over in the past chapters, which is the mature markets, the emerging markets and the less affluent markets, there are different factors that affects the market trends every single day. For example, the people in the mature markets (cities like Sydney, Cape Town in South Africa and San Francisco in California) are mainly driven by *personalization* (choice, flexibility and control) which is about knowing what their needs are and knowing how those needs must be met. They are also driven by *trust*. The world is not as safe as it used to be years back. Many people have been scammed, more especially in this internet controlled world. The people in this markets needs to know if they can trust both you and your business, not only trusting if they can receive the products or services they paid for but also if your products will be able to meet their needs as expected. They are also driven by *convenience.*

Business is no longer about what you are selling but how you are selling it. The people in this markets value time. Their day to day life is faster than elsewhere. They want to know if what you are providing them with can save them time so that they can use that extra time to pursue other things. Most businesses in today's business world have gained so much market share simply because of selling nothing but convenience. Look at big companies like McDonalds that has built multi-billion dollar business ventures out of a business model that simply offered the market a great hamburger meal and coke in exactly sixty seconds in the drive-through and guaranteed you free food if it takes more than a minute.

Let's look at other market, there is the emerging markets. Just like the people living in the mature markets, the people living in the emerging markets have similar needs as well. Think countries like Dubai, cities like Beijing. For me, and maybe other people coming from developing countries like Botswana, a land-locked country surrounded by the fastest growing African economies, I had a very big problem one day when I landed in Johannesburg in South Africa and I tried to come up with a business idea to run in Johannesburg. I couldn't find any. Life there was so fast and very much developed. But one thing for sure, I knew that no matter what I see, there is surely something that anyone who can think better than I do, and probably more exposed than I was to the day to day life of Jo'burg can come up with something that will change how life is lived in Jo'burg. I have been to Hong Kong as well. I will tell you the truth, the only thing I thought of ten minutes after landing in Hong Kong was to package Oxygen for the African tourists that visits Hong Kong. I couldn't breathe. After a few days I was okay. But hey, anything could have happened in those few days before you catch a good breath.

In the emerging markets, the people's needs are mainly driven by personalization and trust, just like those in the mature markets. An emerging market is a country/city that has some characteristics of a developed market, but does not meet standards to be a developed market. This includes countries that may become developed markets in the future or were in the past. But here is the thing, the other driver that has given the business world a new face altogether in this market is *recognition*. Image matters to people living in this market. Brands. Cutting edge technologies. Labels. You name it. As long as your products/services gives somebody that unique sense of achievement, you are the guy.

We also have the less affluent markets. These are the markets that are mostly characterized by people with the lowest income and most of the time their lifestyle resembles lack of innovation, education, growth and development. For most of us who grew up in townships and villages we will find it easy to relate more with this type of market. The world is transforming on daily basis. Because of this transformation, places which has less affluent markets are facing different challenges ranging from connectivity, education, cash flow, development and market access. Most entrepreneurs serving this market often face different challenges with penetrating the market with good quality products/services that the market can afford unlike those in the other types of markets. Here's is what we have to learn, consumption in this market is mostly driven by simplicity, affordability and trust.

The market may not mind using your product/service, but here is the thing, when it is an innovation or any form of technology, before everything else, the bigger question will always be *"can I afford this?"* On top of that, the market will need products and services that has gone through reverse innovation to be made simpler to be used by the people in the community. They also need to be assured that they can be trusted. Many entrepreneurs in the emerging and mature markets has found a very unique opportunity to take the products and services in their markets and 'reverse innovate' them and sell them in the less affluent markets. Isn't it what it is done by the people that are coming to your country to set up businesses in your market? Some people asked me before that, when foreigners come to your country, why is it that they can easily set up successful businesses out of opportunities that were there all the time in front of us and we couldn't see them. Here is the truth, some of these guys are not necessarily creative, they are people from other bigger markets and when they get to our countries they feel the same way you feel when you go to your home village or cattle post.

They don't see the things they are used to back home where they come from, and some of those things they can't live without. And guess what? They go ahead and implement them. And soon enough, we join the 'development'. This is why it is important for you as an entrepreneur to travel the world. Get exposed. See how other people are living their lives in other countries. See how other entrepreneurs are doing business in their markets. Do what these guys do, instead of going to the city to experience the great city life, bring the city life to the village. Having talked about the 3 types of major markets that we discussed, if we are to serve any of these markets, remember, we are in this because we want to solve problems our markets face every day. In other words, if we are to continually be relevant in the market, we must focus on the 'needs' of the people in those markets and see how we can best attend to them. Relevance is our only future-proof strategy for our businesses.

We must think like people who want to play a key role in shaping the future. We need to think like people whose desire is to create solutions that will add value and completely solve big market problems. It doesn't matter where you are in the world, you can be that entrepreneur that the world has long been waiting for. Who would have ever thought that a boy born in Pretoria (South Africa) would grow into a man worth 21 billion USD, celebrated by the world as a business magnate, inventor, investor and engineer. Elon Reeve Musk did it. This man is literally transforming the whole motor industry worldwide. It is true, the people who shake the world are those who think.

This is for you my African fellow entrepreneurs. It is easy to call yourself an entrepreneur. It is easy to look the part and have everybody around you believe that you are an entrepreneur. Calling yourself an entrepreneur does not make you an entrepreneur. Wearing nice suits and taking pictures on hotel lounges and restaurants does not make you an entrepreneur. Our efforts most of the time are channeled towards looking like entrepreneurs and not becoming entrepreneurs. We do what we do in daily basis just to keep up with the image that we have sold to the people. Social media has put us under a serious pressure to want to maintain a certain image. It is very unfortunate that we live in the times when young people in other continents are channeling their energies towards creating globally competitive business ventures and we are just here in Africa satisfied with scoring likes on Facebook.

We want to look like Millionaires and not work hard to become Millionaires. I have friends who are young Millionaires, having spent the little time I have spent with them I have got to learn that; you will not become a millionaire by rolling with Millionaires, you will be a millionaire by doing what millionaires do. There is a type of thinking which everybody who sees himself as an entrepreneur must possess. The difference between the rest of the people and entrepreneurs is nothing but a mindset. It is how we think that causes us to do what we do. Entrepreneurship is about identifying and solving problems.

It is very important that you realize that the success of your business is at the mercy of the quality of your thinking as the business owner. It may be your thinking individually as the pioneer of the business, which is the case with most entrepreneurs, or that of your team. But after all has been said and done, by reason that your business got into existence via the vehicle of thinking, then therefore thinking will keep in alive. Thinking is an action that one must deliberately apply himself or herself to. It is a hard thing to do, that's why a lot of people don't do it. But it is very unfortunate (or fortunate) for us as entrepreneurs that we cannot survive entrepreneurship in the absence of proper thinking. I normally jokingly tell people that there is a very huge difference between thinking and *'recalling'*. A lot of people spend time fantasizing about past memories, and to them, that is thinking. The type of thinking that is our subject of interest here is the one which requires one to travel into the futuristic times to create concepts, ideologies and initiatives which can be implemented now for the benefit of them that requires the benefit of its existence at this present time and in the future.

It is from this point that entrepreneurs think from, that's why they are peculiar because they create solutions which many wouldn't think of, or at least be more passionate about. We live in a very fast paced world. Time is moving very fast. I read a very shocking research few years back that said *"in today's world, information doubles every two years"*. This doubling of information is an ultimate residual effect caused by thousands and millions of trailblazers by virtue of continually innovating solutions to better the lives of humanity around the world. Meaning, what you know now will be irrelevant two years later. The market evolves every single week. The entrepreneurship world has taken the lead in influencing the growth of anything in the world. It has taken the lead in determining the pace at which life is moving in the world. There is always something new somewhere in the market. And the things that hits the market these days are things which brings a complete change to the whole game in the industry.

This is business, when others are busy celebrating the new inventions that they have launched into the market, others are on the other side beginning their mourning season because their businesses had to close because they are no longer relevant to the market and therefore everyone is running after the new kid in the block. Most of the time this happens simply because they never applied themselves to proper thinking which was to expose them to new ways and dimensions of innovation and creativity which was ultimately going to suggest ways in which their business could stay relevant to the market. Let me make this statement right here; *you are not the only one in the market*. You could be the only one in your small corner there, but trust me, someone is somewhere out there in the blues in the same industry with you and he is coming after your market. We live in a global world. We are longer competing with our local folks.

It doesn't matter where you are in the world, when you see yourself launching a business just know that you have entered a global market. You may not be selling anything internationally, or even nationally, in fact, the only people who knows about your business are people in your hood and your friends on social media, but trust me, there is someone out there who is coming after your market with the same business. If you are to be successful in today's entrepreneurship, you need to think like a globally competitive entrepreneur. Of course, there's two parts to it, the side of your mental strength in terms of your psychology as an entrepreneur. Many good books has taught on this subject countless times. But then again, there is the side of your thinking which we are interested in right now which is your creative and innovative thinking abilities.

If we were to throw you into the middle of Texas right now and say *"start a business"*, what would it be about? Listen to yourself right now saying *"Texas?"*, you have just gone blank right now. It's okay, don't worry about it. Let's now say, if we were to throw you into the middle of Singapore and say to you that, run the same business you are now running or planning to do, how were you going to run it? In fact, in how many weeks should we go to our local airport to welcome you back home from your international entrepreneurial experience? The truth is, though many of us desires it, we are not ready for the global market. We think we still have time. Matters worse, we don't even see that before we know it, foreign entrepreneurs would have invaded our local markets with high quality products and services with very good value proposition and very attractive prices and winning all the market to themselves. Which is not wrong. Every entrepreneur (including yourself) would want to see their businesses serving different clients from different far countries someday. What does that really mean? It means you also want to invade the market currently served by the locals of that market. It will be a great success for you if you would manage to do that. In fact, you would have earned yourself some respect in the entrepreneurship world being celebrated as one of the entrepreneurs who have made it internationally and globally.

But why will it be wrong for other entrepreneurs out there just like you to want to serve your market which you are even failing dismally to service? Think entrepreneur - think. In this fast moving world of ever innovative ideas and concepts, where do you see your business in the world in the next 5-10 years? That's easy to tell, what about the next hundred years and beyond? Let me tell you something pioneer, if your business is going to die the day you die then you would have failed dismally as an entrepreneur. Businesses don't survive on inertia mode, they survive and grow because of continuous creative thinking and innovation. The unfortunate part is that, if you choose not to think, your competitors will think and that will be the beginning of your end as a business. The market evolves every week. There are new updates every now and then.

Companies around the world are out there seeking to make the global market better through their own continuous personal development. And what are you doing? If you are used to making sales because people buy just to support you, my friend, you should get ready to have someone next to you selling the same thing you are selling and people will buy what he is selling and not yours simply because they like the product of that person even though they don't even know the owner. Did you buy your iPhone because you love Steve Jobs or because you love iPhones? Is what you are offering the market something that can make a cut by itself in the industry without you having to be in the picture? If it happens right now that somehow you begin to dislike Mark, will you deactivate your Facebook account? Be able to create a business which can continually serve the world even generations to come. But it all comes down to you as the pioneer, are you willing to apply yourself to the proper thinking that other globally competitive entrepreneurs are applying themselves to?

Our problem is that when we create our businesses, particularly our ideas, better put, products and services, we create them with our local market in mind and not the global market. What keeps our ideas and businesses small is not only its administration but also our vision for the business itself. We know what we want to do for the market, but we have no idea when it comes to where exactly are we taking this business to in the later times to come. Our vision for our businesses are short sighted. Our businesses are short-lived because the vision of the business in its smallness had already been exhausted. We need to start creating our businesses with the world in mind. We need to start creating our businesses, our products and services with the global market in mind.

Thinking internationally does not only call you to start thinking putting your products in the shelves of an international store somewhere, it means creating products which if they be put next to other products from international entrepreneurs, yours may still maintain its superiority because it satisfies the competition which exists at international level. Standards my friend, standards. We are not only saying attack other territories, all we are saying is, if yours be attacked, be able to remain the king of the jungle. Simply because you have the required value proposition at the highest level of attractiveness when it comes to pricing. Your level of thinking should resemble that you want your company to be around for a while. The success of your business is at the mercy of the quality of your thinking as its manager. Businesses never grows beyond the thinking ability of them that manage it.

Everything that you see around you has begun first as a thought. It has begun as an idea. Somebody had to come to the realization that there is need for its existence. The phone you are using. The clothes you are wearing. The food you are eating. The shoes you are wearing. Everything, it is all a result of a thought process. Look at everything around you right now and imagine the time when it was being processed in somebody's mind as just a thought. How would you have done it? A lot of entrepreneurs can come to the realization of a very lucrative gap in the market but fail to craft a suitable and sustainable solution for it. Some do manage to come up with some sort of a solution, but fail to either implement it or maintain it. One of the greatest frustrations of being an entrepreneur is having to see your dream die in your eyes because you can't seem to come up with a solution for your solution to work. I've heard one speaker before speaking this words during a seminar, he said, *"things don't end wrong, they start wrong"*.

I believe that the limited thinking which a lot of entrepreneurs excise during the creation of their businesses is responsible for many casualties of businesses. I tell my clients all the time that, look, you got into business because you saw a gap in the market. That simply means that there was someone already serving that market with something that still left a loophole in the market which you managed to identify. If that small loophole is equal to your business and you say that it can generate that much revenue, how much loophole are you willing to leave open when you create your own business? What gives competitors a chance to compete with you is your inability to think things thoroughly. Look, I'm not in any way saying there is a level of thinking which will seal all the loopholes a hundred percent.

Perception is the ultimate reality but it is not the ultimate truth. They say perception determines reception. When you look at your industry, what do you see? When you look at your company, what do you see? What have you heard about your industry? Do you see possibilities? Do you see the end or do you see the beginning? We live in a world which is full of people who tried a few things and failed and they are now in a mission to discourage everyone who is trying to achieve what they failed to achieve. What opinion do you hold about the future of your industry? Do you even see the future of your industry? It matters how you see the mountains before you. It matters how you see the difficulty before you. It matters how you see the hurdles and the challenges before you.

Where other people see impossibilities, you should be able to see possibilities. Dare to make the impossible possible. Enter industries and businesses that people gave up on and build the world's biggest success stories. Go after the big bloated corporations that have been there for long and serve the market with something better that will give you a fair share of their market. You can do this, yes you.

When you have conquered your mind you have conquered your life. When you have conquered your mind you have conquered your business. When you have conquered your mind you have conquered your industry. When you have conquered your mind you have conquered entrepreneurship. We are where we are in our entrepreneurial lifestyle because of what we have done so far simply because of the quality of the decisions we have made thus far.

CHAPTER 8

HOW PASSIONATE ARE YOU?

"It is not the smart that gets ahead in life, it is the bold"

- Robert Kiyosaki

Entrepreneurship is for the crazy. You can't be an entrepreneur and be normal. This journey is for the insane. The bold. You have to be crazy. Literally. To see things that many people don't see, and to believe in the things that are yet to become and still pursue them despite what the world is trying to suggest to you will require a certain level of passion far above the normal. Henry Ford once said *"if I asked them what they wanted they would have said faster horses"*, but he saw a multi-billion dollar automobile industry in the time where not even a single car has been made. This may be old examples of disruption, let's talk about those that are happening right now in our generation. The Elon Musk vision for electric powered automobiles. Or Jessica Mathews' soccket ball. Passion.

Have you ever seen a passionate person? Let me tell you the truth, although it is commitment that keeps one in business, it is the passion that gets one started. Not just passion, but that passion that makes you feel some heat in your chest whenever you talk about your dreams. The type of passion that almost suspends all other senses in your body that you only remember to eat or go to the bathroom only because somebody had to force you to do so. The type of passion that makes you feel like quitting your job to pursue your dreams even though you don't know what's going to sustain your life onwards. It is the kind of passion that keeps a man awake and grinding at the most oddest hours. It is the kind of passion that makes you feel that even when nobody seems to understand what you are trying to achieve you just beat up your chest and ride on a path nobody has ever walked before. The kind of passion that makes you want to pursue your dream no matter how foolish you may seem to those watching your life journey.

People always asked me about where I get my passion. I don't have a more sophisticated answer to the question, but if there's something that I know about passion is that passion is something that up builds with the inspiration that you keep receiving from whatever source you are exposed to. Inspiration is everywhere. Literally. The more you see something that inspires you the more your passion for that thing builds up in you. There is another level of passion which is beyond the goose bumps you get when you see something that resonates with your heart desires, a level which you pursue something out of conviction that calls you to sacrifice your life for what you believe in. A level where it is not about how you feel about that you should do, but only care about getting it done no matter the cost.

How far would you go in your business if you looked at building it like Jesus looked at building his church through offering himself in the cross for the salvation of his people? Are you willing to build your business even if its success will be celebrated by your child long after you have departed from earth? According to my own opinion, our passions are connected to our purposes. Most of the time we use the word '*passion*' and '*purpose*' interchangeably. We use the word to signify what we strongly feel divinely wired to exercise to add value to humanity. Expressing it in goal form as we always do molds it to resemble purpose. When we look a little closer into this, we will see that now passion resembles itself as both the destination and the vehicle that gets you to the destination at the same time. You need passion for you to push until you reach the level of living in the reality of your passion.

A story is told of the ten small birds that were left in a nest on a tree and wanted to fly to the other tree. The teller of the story says that the mother of the ten small birds left them early in the morning while they were still asleep to fetch something for their breakfast. It happened that as they woke up to the beautiful African rich sunrise, birds flying around, butterflies flying around, great melodies of different birds singing and blending together. It was amazing. It happened that as they were watching this beautiful scenery, they saw other small birds flying from their nests to the other big beautiful green tree. Everyone was flying to that tree. They seemed very happy and enjoying life. They would fly very high singing different melodies and performing certain stunts in the air. *"Wow"*, screamed one of the birds that was watching in great awe, his name was Mike. They were astonished. *"I can do that too"*, Mike remarked. *"Whoa, wait, you have never ever flew in your life. Not even once. For as far I'm concerned, we should not leave this nest until mum comes back. Besides, it's dangerous out there. You could die"*, said one of the other small birds. Mike turned and looked at all the birds that were in the nest and said, *"I want to fly to that other tree, I have never done it before, yes, I don't even know how to fly, but I want to fly to that other tree"*. His eye brighten up as he was talking.

Excitement began to build in his heart. He began to run around the next and flipping some little wings of his. The other four birds that were with the rest in the nest began to fall in love with what Mike was doing. They could see possibilities as well. They joined the line and started running with Mike inside the nest. Others were still seating there in nest, afraid. Afraid of the unknown. Afraid to even join the line to at least run around inside the nest. But just like Mike and his crew, something in them was telling them that they can also fly, but because of fear, they chose to do what is more safer; seating in the nest. Mike finally headed towards the edge of the nest, he looked at the other four small birds that were behind him, and he looked at the ones which were just seating there held captive by fear, he winked at them, and he jumped off.

The four birds ran to the edge of the nest to see if indeed he is flying. As they watched, Mike was struggling to flip his wings and he was approaching the ground faster and faster. He was screaming and choking at the same time. He tried to suspend in the air but he couldn't. Mike opened his eyes and he could see the ground getting near and near. His little tiny wings began to feel heavy and painful. He tried to flip them, but he couldn't. He looked at the ground again and he could see rocks he was going to possibly hit his head on. *"What if you die out there?"* the words of his siblings began to ring in his head. The four birds couldn't see him anymore. Tears began to cover their tiny round eyes. Mike looked down again and closed his eyes with the hope not to see himself crushing his head against the rock. As soon as he closed his eyes, he felt a very big wing holding him tight and going up at a very fast speed. When he was getting excited, the wing left him again and he was now headed to the ground again. He flipped the wings one more time.

When he was about to reach the ground the wing came and lifted him up again, *"come on man, you can do this"*, the bigger bird said to him, he flipped the wings one more time, he was getting better and better with flying with his own wings. Mike began to ascend higher and higher. He got very excited. He began to sing his song with his little tiny melodious voice. The big beautiful green tree was now even much closer. He saw other birds coming in and others going out. It was amazing. He flew higher and higher with the other birds that were there at the beautiful tree, birds that were even much older than him. He was now enjoying life.

The four birds that he left at the nest were looking at him from the nest while he was enjoying life in the other tree. They were not just seeing birds, they were seeing a bird that they know. The bird that they were born with. The bird that they were staying with in the same nest. The bird that they were running around with in the nest, just a couple of minutes ago. As they were still watching, Mike took some of the food from the tree and flew back to the nest. As soon as the applause of his grand entrance was over, the mother came in as well, and she asked them. *"Where did you get the food you are eating?"* they smiled, and they all fastened their eyes on Mike. The mother couldn't understand 'how' Mike could possibly give his brothers and sisters that food. She looked at him and said, *"Mike, tell me the truth, did your father come here while I was away?"*, *"No, he didn't"*, responded Mike. The mother asked him again, *"then how did you get this food?"* Mike looked at the mother and said, *"I will show you"*, he winked, and then he ran off and flew away.

The mother ran to the edge of the nest to watch his boy flying, *"wow"*, she busted into tears of joy. *"Come on boys, let's fly"*, she said to the rest of the birds, the four immediately jumped out and flipped their little tiny wings. It was awesome. *"Come on guys, I did it, you can do it too"*, Mike shouted from the other tree.

How passionate are you about your business? If your passion is bigger than your fears, your eyes will begin to see the possibilities. The truth is, taking a step to launch into the atmosphere of your wildest dreams you will need significant amounts of energies emanating from the tanks of your passion. Be passionate.

CHAPTER 9

WHAT IS THE LEVEL OF YOUR PERSEVERANCE?

"A river cuts through the rock, not because of its power but because of its persistence"

Jim Watkins

Entrepreneurship is not for the faint hearted, it is for the brave, the persistent, and the patient and for those who sees overcomers within themselves. I had the privilege to seat one on one with one of Botswana's top richest man in the land, the author of *The Magic of Perseverance*, Dr. Magang at some point in my growth years. It was the best moment of my life. I think that was the richest twenty minutes I have ever had thus far. Considering the fact that millions of people out there are still hoping to one day seat with this wise old man. The captain of perseverance himself. He wrote a lot in his books about perseverance. It was at Mug & Bean in one of Gaborone's best malls called Riverwalk Mall. I was seating there in a meeting with one of my friends. As we were talking with my friend, I couldn't believe my eyes, he came and sat at a table that was next to the one that was next to ours.

I grew up seeing him on newspapers, magazines and television. And he was there, about seven meters away from me, all by himself. I told my friend, *"Hold on, I will be right back"*. So I went to meet him and greeted him and asked if I could seat with him for a few minutes. *"O mosimane wa ga mang mona?"* (Meaning, 'you look familiar, where do you come from'. It's our culture, that's how elderly people will usually greet the youngsters). It was an honor for me that I looked familiar to an international icon). It felt good, although he mistook me for someone else. So I sat down after explaining to him a short biography of my origin. Knowing me, lights on, camera check, sound check, and the talk show had begun. As we were talking, I was astonished as the Bible people were when they were listening to the teaching of our Lord & Savior Jesus Christ.

He began to offload his wisdom to me.

"Entrepreneurship is a journey, just like from here to Francistown. It

is not a one day thing. It has many challenges. Many challenges. But just like any other journey, only those who choose to embark on it to the end will arrive at where the journey leads to. And only those who will make it to the end will enjoy the fruits of their perseverance". I wish you could feel the potency of this statement. In fact, I wish you were there at this meeting to hear it for yourself. He began to elucidate further and said, *"The problem with you young people is that you want overnight successes. You want to start a business today and tomorrow morning you expect it to be pumping millions".* Well, I was guilty of this too at the time, we thank God for the liberation.

I began to think of the words of one of my mentors, BF Rams, I was attending one of his meetings and he said these words when he was talking about *'building a momentum for success',* he said;

"A momentum is a force/strength that is gained by motion or a series of events. An object in motion will remain in motion until it meets resistance. When the power that is driving you becomes lesser than the force resisting you, you will experience stagnation. Many dreamers have become just that. If your dream is real, the proof is action. Everyone in life has a momentum, but here is the thing; where is yours taking you? An average millionaire became a millionaire by running at least 10 companies which didn't work. The difference between winning and failing is the momentum. ***Momentum is deliberately created, consciously grown. Create it deliberately, maintain it intentionally.*** *To create a momentum, one must understand your area of passion and work on it on the law of process. You may start small, but don't lose the vision of your greatness. Leaders and innovators have something in common, they love what they do. By doing what you love doing, you will be personally and financially rewarded while making an impact. Every man will be remembered for their passion or forgotten for the lack of it. Great achievers know who they are and where they are going."*

Entrepreneurship is not easy, at least to many entrepreneurs out there. It shouldn't to be. If it was easy we wouldn't have the Bill Gates, the Strive Masiyiwa, the Patrice Motsepe, the Aliko Dangote, the Mark Zuckerberg, and the Lesang Magang. It requires more than just will, but passion, tenacity, stamina, and determination to reach its level of success. It is a path with gold that can only be seen by you. It is a journey that you should be prepared to embark on even if it means embarking on it alone. It is a journey that will require you to be okay with being laughed at for the longest time possible and declared stupid knowing and believing in your heart that those who are laughed at today because of their vision will be celebrated tomorrow because of it.

This is earth, everything is subject to time. The law of process is there to season the great while weeding out the weak. The magic is not in starting a business, the magic is in staying in the business. The law of process is there to groom, to season, to refine great entrepreneurs. Most of all these businesses that are worth billions today didn't even exist a few years back. They got created by men and women who believed that it will take time, but whatever time it takes, they are willing to do whatever it takes to stay alive to see the day of their greatest success in those businesses. Behind every glory, there is a heart breaking story. The story of perseverance. The story of long suffering. The story of near death experiences. The story of shame and embarrassment. They story of faith. The story of tenacity. You need to learn to persevere to the end. Don't let yourself die with that dream, you have to launch it. You have to pursue it to the end.

CHAPTER 10

LOOK FOR OPPORTUNITIES, THEY WON'T ALWAYS LOOK FOR YOU

"The opportunity of a lifetime must be utilized in the lifetime of the opportunity"

- Boago F. Ramogapi

You need to change the way you think. You need to change the way you see things. Optimism is the foundation of entrepreneurship. It is the bedrock which is anchoring the rigidity of the foundation of entrepreneurship. It is the backbone of entrepreneurship. Where other people see problems and challenges you see opportunities. Haven't you heard that entrepreneurship is the art of meeting a need in the market? You cannot meet the needs in the market if your eyes shows you what the rest of the people see. The beauty of entrepreneurship lies in the ability of entrepreneurs to identify the unpleasant experiences which has disadvantaged countless number of people and turned it into a glorious and very inspirational success story. From your day one in the entrepreneurship world to the last day, you will need to see everything through the lenses of opportunity. If you don't, you will die young because of too much stress and worry. You will miss out on so many opportunities that came your way that could have turned your business into a multi-billion dollar company.

You need to develop a habit of being what people call a *'go-getter'*. You have to inculcate and construct within you an attitude that says *'if it doesn't happen, I'm going to make it happen'*. Look, the world is not the way most of us would desire it to be. Opportunities in the business world are everywhere, but they will not always knock on your door as you would expect them to. You need to be determined to pursue opportunities. There are some doors in business which will only open to those who will not give up knocking on them until they open. There are some deals which will only be signed by men and women who are willing to put in an extra effort on top of the bare minimum requirements. The business is not in your office. The business is not in your warehouse. The business is not in your house. The business is out there in the streets.

The business is out there in other people's offices. The business is in other people's warehouses. The business is out there in other people's houses. You need to go out there and get it for your business. Did you know that some people don't know that you exist? I don't only mean your company, I also mean you the entrepreneur.

The problem with most of us is that we think we have second chances. Not all of us gets second chances. We walk through life taking opportunities we see for granted. We don't know that some golden moments comes once in a lifetime. We need to embrace the mentality that embraces opportunities that crosses paths with ours. You need to understand that as far as life is concerned, you don't deserve anything. If you are to have something meaningful in your life you need to place a fervent demand on what you want. Even though many fervently and passionately pursue after these opportunities, they still don't get them, those who do utilizes them to the maximum. Now imagine the same opportunities many seek after but can't find them, those same opportunities presents themselves before you effortlessly but you still take them for granted.

Right now, many entrepreneurs are crying for funding across Africa, but did you know? Over P120 million ($12million) is set aside for funding young entrepreneurs in Botswana by the Ministry of Youth through the *Youth Development Fund*. The government has already spent approximately 1 Billion Pula on funding start-ups. But many entrepreneurs in Botswana are still relaxed and they don't want to utilize these great blessings. There is so many opportunities around us but we pretend not to see them. Somebody once said that *"in today's generation, if you want to be a millionaire, all you need to do is will it and work a little bit harder and in less than a year you will be a millionaire"*. It took some even months.

There's a legion of opportunities everywhere for you. The world is a place full of opportunities for everyone. But let me say this, soon enough, all these opportunities that we are toying with will one day cease to be, more especially opportunities in Botswana for young people. And that's when most of us are going to see how valuable they were and how blessed we were to be nationals of Botswana at the time. I want to urge you, the best time to utilize that opportunity is today. The only time you can utilize the opportunity of a lifetime is in the lifetime of the opportunity. Keep in mind that like it has been said numerous times before, *"when preparation meets opportunity, greatness is birthed"*. Always live ready to utilize every right opportunity that comes your way in the lifetime of that opportunity.

CHAPTER 11

WIPE YOUR LENSES

"Go as far as you can see, you will see further"

- Peter Mbada

A certain young lady who was blind once said, *"The greatest tragedy in life is not losing sight, the greatest tragedy in life is having sight and not have vision"*. The problem with a lot of entrepreneurs today is not money, it is not resources, but vision. We have touched on this issue in the previous chapters and we will still continue to engage this topic in the next chapters. Entrepreneurship in our today's times is far beyond just creating a solution, but it is about creating sustainable solutions which should be subject to continuous development to remain relevant across multiples of generations to come.

Visionaries plan not because they have money, they plan because they have a vision. They say a vision has within itself the ability to attract its own provision. A lot of people are stranded in their businesses because all they had in mind when they got into business was their product and not the vision of the product. How far can you see? How clear is your vision? The greatest frustration in business is not knowing what you should do.

Your vision should not fit into your budget, your budget should fit into your vision. If you want to go far in your entrepreneurial journey, this is an understanding that must dominate your mental faculties as an entrepreneur. People remain small because their moves are calculated within the resources they see with their naked eyes. One of the entrepreneurs that I followed very closely from church when I was growing up, Mr. Bathusi Malope once told me these words that I will never forget, he said, *"My brother, always plan like you have all the money in the world"*. From that day, that's what I have been doing. Planning without mental limitations helps you tap into the world of possibilities. You begin to see things that a lot of your competitors don't see. You begin to see things that will set you apart. Faith is what you need. You need to believe. Your convictions has to be your driving force. It has to be the fuel that keeps you going. It can only drive you when there is a journey to be taken, a journey from a visible now to a foreseeable future. Be led from the inside.

The day you see yourself bigger than your vision, know that you don't have a future. The vision has to be the one that carries you, not the other way round. We grow into destiny, destiny doesn't grow into us. When you don't have a vision you will be led by people who do. The world belongs to them that has a clear vision of what they are doing and where they are willing to go. The world is shaken by the people who think. Industries are led by people who think. Industries are led by people who are driven by vision. It doesn't matter who their competitors are, they will always consistently thrive into the future as a force to be reckoned with. Your competitors will never be shaken by what you are currently doing, they are shaken by what you are willing to do in the future. Vision secures future territories. The people who are currently leading industries today didn't wake up today leading industries, they began leading them through a vision that they carried from their day one.

One of the greatest stories of our time that really inspires me even today, it is the story of the evolution of Dubai. From a desert country sustained by fish and oil to the most beautiful tourist attraction city full of unique mega structures that doesn't exist anywhere else in the world. All these under a strong vision of a man who choose to follow his convictions. A man who chose to dare to dream, to set himself up for a journey to do exploits and create long lasting monuments that didn't only sound impossible but improbable to many. He inspires me a lot. He had me believing that it is indeed real and not just a mere mantra or a maxim that we declare occasionally that 'there is nothing I cannot do'. It is through this man, who goes by the name *Sheikh Mohammed Bin Rashid Al Maktoum* that I chose to dare to dream and not just dream but dream big.

I may be born in Windhoek in Namibia as the 22nd born child of my father, raised by a single mother in a small village called Mahalapye in Botswana in a big poor family, but that doesn't mean that I cannot create things that will even attract the attention of the world. I don't know about you, but I believe that your vision regardless of your current situation is possible. Faith always settles the matter. One of the things that I have learnt from him that I am using even today in my life is his habit of laying out his vision illustrated through prototypes. It is one thing to see the vision in your head through your imagination but it is another to see it physically illustrated either throw drawings, sketches, or even through documentation. As an entrepreneur, one of the things you need to pay close attention to is the fact that you don't work alone but you work with other people who were not there when you got the inspiration to follow that dream. They are not the ones with the vision but yourself.

Be that as it may, it is of great importance for both of you to pull together with great energies to realize the dream. But here is the thing, unless and until they see the vision from your vantage point, your efforts in going forward will always be compromised. They need to be sold out to the vision. The only way for them to be sold out to the dream is when they have the same or similar conviction that you have, and the only way for them to have that conviction is when they also see what you see. This is why now it is very imperative for you to sell the vision to them by all means possible. But now the problem is, we have leaders of businesses that can't even see where they are going. And like Jesus has said in the Bible, *"if a blind leads a blind, the two shall fall into the pit"*. Wipe your lenses, see better and lead better.

Money is not your mission. Money without vision will lead to your destruction. The bottom line of every business might be profitability, but money should never be the mission. See money as an indicator in your business. When the money is good, your business is functioning properly. When the money is low, there is something you are doing wrong. When money is average, you are performing at average. Money is there to fuel your mission, it is not your mission. These are the words I have heard Bishop TD JAKES saying in a video before. *"Money makes things possible. Money breaks limitations. Money makes things easy. But hey, money is not the mission"*. Look, if your products and services truly adds value like you claim they do, they will definitely be used by people. And you know that usage comes with bucks. Focus on adding value and improving your solution. That's your mission. The day you see yourself pursuing money more than value addition, know that you have seized being an entrepreneur, you are a business man.

Ask yourself this question; as we speak right now, what's in your budget list? And how many of those things will advance your vision? Entrepreneurs struggles a lot. They struggle because they know that what they see inside them is bigger and better than what they see in the outside. There is a burning desire to turn their dreams in to reality. They are about one thing and one thing only, and that's building their dream. They see every penny and every thebe they get as a brick to advance their goal and nothing else seem more worthy of their cent than their goals. Look at yourself right now, is the person I'm describing the person that you are? If not, now is the time, you know what to do. Let your vision reflect in your budget list. Look at it this way, the lack of vision prioritization in your life marks the end of whatever it is you are trying to do.

CHAPTER 12
AFRICA

"Our children may learn about heroes of the past. Our task is to make ourselves articles of the future"

- Jomo Kenyatta

Africa's population as we speak has now exceeded 1.216 billion, it has been projected that by 2050, the bulk of the world's population will take place in Africa, of which 1.3 billion of the 2.4 billion additional people expected between 2015 and 2050 will be added to Africa. How is your vision reflecting your readiness or at least your willingness to contribute towards serving this development? It is easy to answer questions like *"where do you see your business in 10 years?"* during interviews, but be that as it may, just between the two of us, are really sure that what you are envisioning for your business relevant to what the world will be in the same timeframe you have set for your vision? Do you even know where the world is going? There are major transformations that are taking place around the world led by different industries but with the technology industry at the forefront. Whether you know it or not, ready or not, these transformations will affect your business.

You may not be interested in going out to reach the world with your business but hear you me, there are millions of other entrepreneurs out there coming to you with theirs. Soon enough, if you are in the same industry with them and you are not willing to think like they do they will automatically swallow you and your market up. This is the reality in other countries, more especially developed countries that big companies swallow up other companies through either acquiring them or choking their ability to serve the market. You may have witnessed it from afar, but if you stay a little longer in business, you will witness it closer, maybe with your business or industry as the subject on the plate. Start today, think. Think proper. How can you become un-buyable? Look, you have the same chance right now to grow into a big globally competitive business, no matter what you have heard complainers say.

Africa is like an orphan child who was left with a fortune by his parents.

He was raised by people who admired the inheritance left for him. He was a child, he didn't know how valuable his inheritance is. Some people would normally come and take some of his inheritance to help themselves but he would not mind because he is a child, he can't understand the value of his inheritance. He takes it for granted that he has a great inheritance. He mourns that he lost his parents while he was very young, he feels like someone should be the one to do everything for him. He is a child, it is understandable. But wait, this child is growing by the day. He learns from other children. He sees other children exchanging their gifts for money and he says to himself, *"I have that too"*. He is still afraid to exchange his, he is a child, we understand, he has never done that before. Oh he could sing, he could dance, he could act, he is so handsome, he can think, he is rich. But no one has ever told him all these growing up, so even when he hears it from other people he is shy to believe it. But Africa is growing. Soon, the world will know that he is Africa, the handsome smart rich boy.

There is knowledge, skills and discoveries indigenous to Africans but people from outside Africa are the ones who are benefiting more from them while we seat here murmuring and grieving over it. We value other people's things because ours are not 'western' or 'eastern' enough. Open your eyes, the world is getting richer and richer every day, and guess who the sponsor is? It is not time to fight people from foreign countries, it is time to see how best we can fairly partner and change the world. I'm looking forward to a day when partnerships shall be erected in the world by young people from different countries around the world to form big globally competitive corporations that will change lives around the world. Big corporations which shall be within themselves platforms that will channel other businesses from one side of the world to the other, by young people through young for the young people. A day when Africans shall not look at themselves as victims but key players in the developments changing lives around the world. Entrepreneurship knows no skin colour, it knows no demography and it knows no geography. It is a world of principles and principles are not a respecter of persons. Any man who shall subject himself to those principles, behold that man shall prosper in his entrepreneurial journey.

It's time to make the world to walk through the streets of Africa. Instead of producing to export our cream to other "better" continents, we need to produce and attract the world, we need to produce and invite the world to come and have the experience of their lifetime. We need to start believing in Africa. Literally. We have the reason to believe even the more. We have so many globally celebrated African entrepreneurs that have proven beyond reasonable doubt that a child born and bred in Africa can start a business from scratch in Africa and grow to be a globally competitive entrepreneur, not just that but even become a billionaire. I've had the privilege to meet the founder of Forbes Africa, Chris Bishop, when he came to Botswana for the Botswana Stock Exchange conference, later on as I was browsing through some books at some book store in town, I saw a very powerful book that he published. In the book he published Africa's Billionaires. I grew up inspired by some of them, I got to learn about others in his book. If you can please grab a copy of his book, I can assure you that you will be greatly inspired.

Africa has many inspirational entrepreneurs who are a testament that you can also make it here in Africa. Here is some of the success stories of African billionaires that was published by Chris Bishop;

The current richest man in Africa, Aliko Dangote.

The young Tsar of Dar, Mohammed Dewji

The $600-million-a-year rent collector, Sudhir Ruparelia

The Capitalist Crusader, Herman Mashaba

The Mining Millionaire and barefoot dreamer, Tim Tebeila

The sage elder of Africa who studied with Mick Jagger, Pascal Dozie

The Three Wise Men, Grey, Robertson and Brozin

From barefoot to a $500 million African media empire, Reginald Mengi

How the mouse are the elephant, Stephen Saad

The king of diamonds, Nicky Oppenheimer

The immigrant priest who became a steel baron, Narendra Raval

From cheap clothes to diamonds, Christo Wiese

Of wine, women and wrong, Wendy Appelbaum

Court battles and 'no' to corruption - a Tour dear Strive, Strive Masiyiwa

Right place, wrong business, right time, Patrice Motsepe

A voyage of discovery, Adrian Gore

'I want to be a billionaire - tonight', Abdulsamad Rabiu

In almost every interview these great people have ever done, none of them has ever denied that they started from nothing. None of them has ever denied that it was hard. Imagine yourself collecting $600 million passive income on annual basis. Imagine yourself having the mines to yourself. Imagine yourself one day being declared *'The richest man/ woman in Africa'*. The dream you have is relevant and it is possible. That African dream that makes you feel you can change the world can indeed one day change the world. From the smallest families of the smallest villages often comes the greatest of the greatest. It is possible that you could be reading this book just like any of these guys read some when they were at your level not knowing that a few years later their lives will be studied by millions of people around the world seeking to build the same legacies they have built. What if a few years from now authors around the world will be profiling your business successes? Don't be amongst the millions of people around the world who just believes that it is possible for anyone to become a billionaire, be the one to believe that 'that billionaire' can be you. Yes you, an unknown African child!

Have you ever heard about Jessica O. Matthews? Jessica is one of the greatest young women Africa has ever had. Born in Nigeria, at 19 years old, the world's best journalists were already blogging about her. Jessica, a tech-guru, the founder and CEO of *Uncharted Play*, whose story is such a great inspiration around the world. The story tellers says that it happened that Jessica visited her home village back in Nigeria during the vacations as it was the norm. She was studying in America at the time. When she got to the village, she found out that electricity was so scarce that if there was any device or gadget that needed power they had to be powered by a diesel generator. This challenge had disadvantaged the lives of people in the village, more especially the students. They couldn't read or study from the evening onwards because it got dark faster. *"You can imagine the hours that these kids were losing every single day of their lives simply because there was no light"*, Jessica remarked during an interview about her company.

The generator, with all the great work of producing electricity to power the village that it was doing, it was also producing so much smoke that affected Jessica's health. She coughed very hard during her visit there. When she told her friends and family in the village about her experience, and dissatisfaction, they just said to her, *"oh yeah, this is the village, girl, you will get used to it like everybody else"*. She refused to conform to the norm. She went ahead to find the best alternatives to power the village. The story teller says that Jessica went back to America and took a soccer ball. She designed some power generation mechanism that will produce power out of kinetic energy. She put it inside the ball and went to the village and gave it to the boys to play with it.

The ball was designed in a such a way that as the boys were kicking the ball around the pitch, the mechanism inside the ball is busy producing and storing the electricity that the homes around the village will use to power their lights and other appliances at night. She called the ball *Soccket Ball.* This was a great game changer. The beginning of the best energy solutions in the world. Straight from Africa by an African young girl. Some of you know her and you once went to school with her or even played with her. Jessica embodies a great vision to power almost everything chargeable with this technology. It is patented, you can't steal it.

The story teller continued to say that Jessica is looking forward to put the same technology in luggage bags so that as you pull it to anywhere, it is busy producing enough power to charge your phone and your laptop during your trips. She is looking forward to also put the technology in different malls under the floor tiles to power the shopping malls as a huge number of people move around the malls. She is looking forward to do great exploits in the energy sector worldwide. *"We want to generate power out of everything that moves"*. This is just the beginning. An African young woman.

CHAPTER 13

WHAT DO YOU HAVE?

"It's not resources but resourcefulness that ultimately makes the difference"

-Tony Robbins

I've met a lot of people before during our coaching sessions, seminars and sometimes during my social media engagements who always told me that they want to start their businesses but they can't because they don't have the finances. During the first *Pioneers MegaFest* that my team and I hosted in Gaborone, the one we had hosted one of South Africa's youngest Millionaires Prince Mazibuko, one of the speakers who was speaking during the seminar, Thabiso Bogopa, made a very powerful statement, he said *"The major problems that Africa's entrepreneurs are facing are not merely economic but psychological, there is need for us to issue out a psychological reform to de-culture, inculcate and construct within African entrepreneurs a mindset that is prosperity and progress orientated"*. Many of us are sitting on so much gold and we can't see it.

We are sitting on so many opportunities but we are still stuck like a lost man in a desert inside a foreign country. We have preoccupied our minds on things that we don't have than the ones that we do have. Our limitations as entrepreneurs and people in general are not necessarily influenced by how deficient our resources are but how deficient our minds are when it comes to being resourceful. The truth of the matter is, there are thousands of other entrepreneurs out there who started off in far much worse conditions than you are but despite all odds they have made it through until they are now considered inspirational icons by many.

Entrepreneurship is about doing more with less. I remember one time when I was given an opportunity to do a presentation at some workshop I was invited to speak at in South Africa, I believe I have shared it also on my social media platforms as well, I said, *"optimism is the backbone of entrepreneurship. We need to learn as entrepreneurs to look at everything through the lenses of opportunity"*. You cannot call yourself an entrepreneur when you still look at challenges as limitations. What gives you a strong backbone in business is your ability to keep the grind going even when everything around you proves that you are headed towards a possible total failure.

You need the mindset which will help you to remain the last man standing who still believes that deep down in the dark hole you are digging there is a giant rock of gold and diamond inside. You need the tenacity to keep pushing even when you don't have the required resources for the job. Trust me, in your line of business, there will always be competitors who will be more resourced than you are bidding for the same job you also want to bid in. It doesn't matter who you are or where you are coming from, there is always going to be something you don't have. The magic is not in waiting to acquire more to be able to start, the magic is in being to start with the little that you have.

I remember one time when I was trying the social media management market, I went to this other big guy and told him about the business that I have which manages social media accounts of big companies. Yes, it was its first day of operation. Zero experience. Zero resources. Zero background. Zero portfolio. Zero everything. But I looked at him and pitched to him a business which sounded like has been kicking some butt in the industry for a while. Well, I never told him that my business has been kicking some butt, he just assumed. I'm very good with that. You should also, otherwise you will lose all the time even when you have all the weapons you need for the war they are recruiting warriors for. So the guy called in one of his assistants, the assistant was responsible for the marketing affairs of the company. It was still a newly established company but already serving big clients, so they had not yet setup departments and all of that.

The guy called me to his office, when I got there he just asked me to confirm if I will be able to make it to their staff meeting tomorrow morning at 7am. *"Yes Sir, I will be there"*, that's me responding to the call I never knew what I'm getting myself into. Like they say, *"today is tomorrow of yesterday"*, so the day came. When I got into the meeting, right there inside a well-furnished boardroom, men and women properly dressed to the occasion, with *O3* water and some endermint sweets on the table, projector screen displaying some graphs I never knew what they were trying to say, *"please wait here"*, some good looking young lady suggested.

So I was waiting outside the boardroom. Looking at a group of experts through their transparent glass walls as they were discussing with serious faces. I sat there, thinking to myself, *"What have I gotten myself into?"* The moment I saw the guy who seemed like he was the last to pitch seating down, I knew that *"e chaile"* (it is show time). The only thing I remember is seeing that good looking young lady smiling at me and pointing me towards the direction of the boardroom door. I walked in there with heavy legs and shaking knees. Mind you, I've never been in this kind of meeting before. The only thing I've done in the past was running my NGO (ALBRIMO) which held its meetings under trees and in school classrooms at the time. I remember seeing a giant suited dark man with glasses trying to introduce me. Everything in the boardroom was blurred except the guy who was speaking. *"So you in a good position to do this job?"* The old man who seemed like the owner of the business asked.

I began to picture my hinge broken laptop whose battery can only last for 30 minutes. The knowledge of how sometimes I can wait for about ten minutes just so that it can open the file explorer gave me a blow in the eye. I remembered that I fell in love with social media management after seeing some guy doing it. I'm talking about a guy who had three Apple Mac computers in his executive office. In that ten seconds of processing this heavy information which I bought with an impression that I'm clearing my throat, I felt that I should just kneel down and apologize to this noble gentlemen who only wanted to give me a chance because I made them feel like I'm worth it. My eyes became hot and almost teary, my heart beating double kicks, my throat beginning to feel like there is something inside trying to choke me, my hands sweating. *"Of course, I will do it. Money back guarantee if you are not satisfied with my work"*. I took it. In less than five minutes of our meeting, the old man shook my hand in agreement.

I don't even remember what the good looking young lady said when I got out of that boardroom. I felt like I've just won a free ticket to jail. My goodness. Look, maybe you don't know, I took that job because weeks before then I spent my entire time knocking office to office trying to get a gig and I was turned down because I didn't have the portfolio. I hated it, I really hated it. I could even sense it every time when I was pitching to a different person when they are about to pop out the question, *"oh nice, so who have you done or for before?"* I'm not the only person who have gone through this. Countless numbers of entrepreneurs out there have gone through it too. Some are going through it now as you are reading this portion of this book. Some will be going through it tomorrow, next week and even years to come.

How many opportunities have you lost simply because you seem to not be having some experience or resource requisite for the job? Look, for as long as everybody is turning you down, you will never have that portfolio. It is not about what I have, it is about what I'm able to do with what I have. I swear a lot of underground producers in the music industry can do far much better job than these so called big studio producers. A lot of people out there can cook far much better than these well-known restaurant. I know a certain lady, very good looking also, she is an accountant by profession but she is an anointed chef. My God. These lady can bake some muffins you will have to take off your shoes so that you can enjoy the fullness of her soothing taste. Many restaurants have nothing on that lady. I'm telling you. When it comes to cooking chicken meat, whether grilling, boiling, and frying or whatsoever, these lady was seriously anointed. Look, there are chefs and there are Chefs.

One day she invited me over to her house and she prepared the chicken meat for me. As we were chatting, I asked her. *"Do you know that Nandos, Chicken Licken, KFC and CFC all serve chicken?"* She looked at me, she chuckled and said, "Yes, that's obvious". I asked her, *"But what's the difference between these guys?"* She said, *"They serve different recipes of chicken"*, I said to her, *"Exactly, just like you, and this is the only backbone of their business, the recipe."* That's all. There's nothing else they are special about. Only their way of cooking chicken meat. *"And you are here seating on a very good recipe for chicken meat, in fact, you are seating on a potential competitor of these guys"*. Of course, she gave the excuse of not having money to start a big restaurant to serve her chicken. I asked her, which is what I'm good at, asking questions, (maybe is because my name is a question, just maybe), *"have you read the biography of Mr. Kentucky?"*, *"No, not yet"*. I looked at her, I remembered the words of our Lord Jesus Christ which the Bible records that he uttered at some point during his earthly ministry, he said, *"my children are perishing because of lack of knowledge"*. The question is, do you know that everything big starts small?

A great man was born as a little boy. A huge elephant was born as a small elephant. Bushy beards started off as just one beard. *"Well, they say go big or go home"*. Sit down, let me tell you, thinking big does not necessarily mean that you should start big. I'm not disputing that there are people who have started big, at least we think they did. The vision may be big, which it should, but you need to understand that its implementation process has its beginning point. Even when you are writing a book, it does not matter how big it is going to be, but you still need to narrow it down to its first sentence you are going to be starting with. We are living in a generation which many call the 'microwave' generation. We want quick results and we want them now. We want to be Millionaires and Billionaires and we want to be those right now.

We have failed to appreciate the fact that the life we are living is a long journey. We are like a bride whose only interest is limited to the limelight of the wedding day forgetting that there is still a long marriage years to prepare for. We want a glorious marriage but we do not want to go through the process of working for it. I will tell you why a lot of people today still haven't launched their business ideas. I will tell you why they think they need millions to start and that's why they haven't started because they don't have that kind of money. The problem is not the resource deficiency, the problem is deficiency in strategic planning knowledge.

Most of us are not acquainted with growing things. We like the results of the processes but we don't like the processes of the results. I've had a conversation with a certain South African forex trader and he told me that he wanted to be a Millionaire when he started. What inspired me the most it was when he told me that he realized sooner that it was not going to take him the short time he thought it was going to take him. From selling his cellphone for Two Thousand Rands and opening a $150 live account, he pressed on day and night every week patiently trading and growing it until it became $100'000, that was his first million Rands. It took him two full years and a half. You need to give up the thought that it is going to be that big sooner. It depends, my point is, and you need to prepare for the growth period of your business. Every big thing had its own small beginning, most of the time small beginning. This is why the Bible says, *"Do not despise the days of small beginnings"*. I like the other statement from the Bible which says *"though your beginning may he small, your end shall be greater"*. It doesn't matter how you start, what matters is that you have started. And that's what you need to focus your energies in, starting.

Anything you have is enough for you to start. Trust me, whether you believe in God or not, he has availed something to everyone enough for him/her to start. If you could look around you right now, there's something in your surrounding which can help you start. That is why I said, optimism is the backbone of entrepreneurship, it is in our ability to look at everything through the lenses of opportunity. What do you see around you? You want to open a music studio, what do you have around you? You want to cook for people, what do you have around you? You want to open a car wash, what do you have around you? You want to host a huge event, what do you have around you? Whatever you want to do, there is something in your possession that you can use to start. In the meantime, it could make a huge progress than you think. Yes, it is not the ideal equipment but it could do in the meantime. What matters the most is that you have started.

Entrepreneurship will always find its way of testing our faithfulness. Entrepreneurship is a call for stewardship. We celebrate all the great entrepreneurs that we celebrate today because they have managed to grow their businesses to where we see them today. And that's the keyword there, grow. All of these guys started from somewhere. Facebook is worth Billions today but it started from a laptop probably worth less than $200 in a dorm room. It started off with very few people and grew from there to now having over one billion users around the world. Mark doesn't have to know you for you to use his business, in fact, he never came to your country and plead with you to join his business. In fact, it is now running and growing because you want it to. If he could decide to close it down, you are going to want to stop him from doing that. Isn't that what you want for your business? It's possible, but you need to start today with what you have.

CHAPTER 14

BE FAITHFUL IN THE LITTLE, YOU WILL HAVE MORE

"Little by little, a little becomes a lot"

- Tanzanian proverb

What will inspire other upcoming entrepreneurs about your business is not what you have achieved but how you have achieved it. One day they will be in the same condition that you are in right now. Having huge dreams that could literally shake the world. But they will need to know how to maneuver through their challenges in pursuit of their dreams. And as a well-established entrepreneur (speaking of the future you), you will need to share your experiences with them such that they don't only get motivation but an idea of how they can deal with their own challenges . Now, imagine yourself in a situation where you have no idea how you got where you did. Let's say we get a chance to seat with Bill Gates and we ask him how he made it, and he has no idea how Microsoft grew to this point. You need to keep in mind as we have already mentioned earlier that entrepreneurship is a call to stewardship.

Stewardship is the ability to take a good care of something as it grows. The only reason why entrepreneurs keep waking up every morning to their offices is because they want to keep the dream alive. The magic is not in starting the business but in keeping the doors of the business open and growing. The growth of every business is in different phases. We grow from one level to the other. We grow from one dimension to the other. We began as aspiring entrepreneurs, became starters, to growers and we are headed towards being premiere entrepreneurs. We are headed towards having our businesses as globally competitive business ventures. We are headed towards owning business ventures that runs without us having to be there. Yes, it is possible. *"A journey of a thousand miles begins with a single step"*. But again as entrepreneurs we need to prove our faithfulness every step of the way. You need to prove right now that you are able to kick-start this business right now with the little resources you have at your disposal.

Resources can be anything; money, equipment, contacts, people, time, etc. You need to prove that you can grow $10 to $1000. That is the only way to know that you can be a Millionaire. At some point in your entrepreneurship journey, you are going to be working with investors. When I was doing my business management course at university one of my favorite lectures there taught me something that I will never forget, she said *"the role of the management is to maximize the shareholder's wealth"*. It doesn't sound deep. It doesn't have to. But that's what our entrepreneurship journey is ultimately leading us to. There are going to be people who are going to be interested in buying a stake in your business. For some, your business is going to require you to engage a few investors. That is when you are going to appreciate the value of proper stewardship. That is when you are going to see why it was necessary for you to be in the situation you are in right now regarding starting or growing your business. You cannot manage a million dollars business if you can't manage a thousand dollars business.

The reason why I love entrepreneurship is that it has within itself the ability to educate you about itself. Whether you went to school for it or not, principles are principles, you going to have to learn them. One way or the other. But do not be dismayed, as hard as it sounds, that's the beauty of entrepreneurship. The adventurous moment of figuring out your way out of complex situations. Remember, you are not just the business owner, you are the CEO, and you are the leader. If you hire people, they will all be looking at you for direction. You can't dodge this job, you better accept it now. People call it management, I like calling it stewardship. What you have right now is enough. Prove that you are the entrepreneur that you say you are.

There was a time when we were running our Launchit program called *'The Project124'*. It is a program we have developed to season aspiring entrepreneurs into real entrepreneurs. I gave all the participants (about twenty seven of them) an assignment. I gave them a task to look for P10 (equivalent to one US Dollar). When they have all found the ten pulas, I gave each and every one of them another task to multiply the P10 as many times as they can through the buying and selling process. Each participant had the maximum of seventy-two hours (72 hours) to do so. It was Sunday evening and the countdown began the next day, Monday morning. Each participant was to record each and every single move they make in the process. When the 72hours had elapsed, each other 27 participants submitted their returns. It was so amazing and shocking at the same time when I reviewed their scorecards. Of course some of the participants brought back the P10 attached to a list of all the excuses why they didn't manage to multiply it. Some brought back P15, P27, some brought over P150 and the one that really inspired me was the young lady who brought back P1'450 (one thousand four hundred and fifty). I couldn't believe it. It was around 4:30 in the evening and I remember seating in my office wondering to myself, *"Did this young girl make this amount of money with my idea?"* I couldn't believe it. But hey, she did. It is not about how much you have in your hands but it is about how much you have in your head.

The idea is not to win because you had all the weapons you needed for the battle, the idea is to conquer the battle even in the midst of hopelessness and confusion with the little that you have. It is in moments like this where the difference between heroes and sissies becomes crystal clear even to a blind man. God specializes in moments like this. Where it seems like nothing is going to come out, where everything shows that you going to fail. Your head will also tell you that you going to fail. People WILL tell you that you WILL fail. But God will tell you that *"I've got your back"*. It's up to you now to man up, and face the situation. You choose who you want to believe, the big situation or the BIG GOD. Hear me, even the heroes you know experienced fear in the midst of the challenges they overcome. Get it from me. But the main thing here now is, what are you going to do with Goliath? It's either he dies or you die, whatever you do God has to be glorified and your death can't glory him.

You need to believe him when he says *"I will deliver your enemies into your hands"*. Hear me and hear me twice, He will deliver your enemies into your hands. How it don't matter. What are you facing now? What if I told you that the little stone in your hand is all that is needed to knock Goliath down? Fear not, call him a giant and you will fear him and die, or call him an uncircumcised Philistine and his head will be equal to that little stone in your hand and you will knock him down and he will die. God is on your side. Arise & Shine!

You will be surprised how much wealth the little coins in your pocket can make you over a number of years. Or the laptop in your house. Or the microwave in your kitchen. Or even the oven in your kitchen. Talk about your own cellphone. Or the space behind your yard. I've heard of this little but great story while I was still at high school at *Gaborone*

Secondary School (GSS). I was part of a class which was dominated by people who were seeing themselves as business owners and industry leaders in the near future (which is slowly becoming a reality), we called ourselves the Cash Money Class. Well, one day as we were chatting after they introduced me to *Rich Dad Poor Dad,* one of the guys that we were with shared a story with us. I can't remember very well who it was. He said, one day as a certain little boy was on his way to school (born from a very poor family), he saw a money clip on the ground. He picked it, a gold new money clip. He didn't know what it was, so because it was a shiny piece of metal, he took it to school with him. As he was in class, still looking at this cute little piece of metal, some girl from his class (one of the rich girls in school) asked him, *"can you give me that?"*, He said *"No, it's mine, I like it"*. The girl replied and said, *"I will give you a pen, a multicolor pen"*.

The thought of owning a multicolor pen got him thinking, and excited. He has never owned one before. He only saw it rich kids only. So he agreed. They battered the pen and money clip. The little boy went home with the pen. Tomorrow morning at school again, during break time, the little boy was just seating next to the tap, one of the rich boys came and said to him, *"can I have that pen"*. He said, *"No, it's mine, I love it"*. The rich boy said, *"Okay, I will give you 2 dollars for it"*. He paused, in his heart he said, *"What? 2 dollars, wow"*. He had never had two dollars before. He traded. The little boy fell in love with possessing things that people will often times want him to give to them for some form of value in exchange.

He went and bought sweets to sell in the school. The two packets of sweets he bought he sold them and bought four more packets. He sold them all. He went and bought packets of peanuts. He sold them like fat cakes. He was now owning 100% market share of the school. He got some other students in other schools to sell for him and earn commission. He went on to negotiate a kiosk space in his school. He stocked different things, pies, toiletries, biscuits and many other things. The school kiosk grew into a community tuck-shop. He opened a few more community tuck-shops around his community. By the time he joined his junior high school, he was financially stable and taking care of himself. He didn't even look like he grew up without parents. By the time he finished his high school, his tuck-shops had turned into a chain of department stores. From a money clip.

CHAPTER 15

ATTRACT THE INVESTORS, SEDUCE CUSTOMERS

"People do not buy goods and service. They buy relations, stories and magic"

-Seth Godin

They say that in seduction, it is the words that undresses you. If you get to think about it, it makes a lot of sense. Every now and then you are going to find yourself having to talk to a lot of different people about your business. No man is an island. You cannot achieve your entrepreneurial goals alone. First from starting the business, getting partners and clients, you going to have to talk to them. In other words, until and unless you talk to them, there is no way you can get them onboard. It is your responsibility to learn proper ways of communicating your vision to the people. I heard some speaker before quoting the words that says *"good marketing makes the company looks smart, but great marketing makes the customer feel smart."*

The reason why you believe so much in your business is because there is an image that you can see in your imagination which keeps you awake at night thinking about it. It inspires you so much that every time you imagine it everything seem possible to you. You feel like you can change the world. And you are right, you can indeed change the world, but you are going to need the world to help you to change it. You going to need some people to help you to pursue the success of that dream. There's a team to build. There are clients to fish. And most importantly, there are investors to get onboard to pump money into your business. There are businesses you can start without investors, but some you going to need some investors from the onset. Either way, even if you can start by yourself, which is even greater, you are still going to need some investors along the way to make your impact in the world a lot bigger that the one you can build by yourself.

For anybody to be inspired by your idea the way you are inspired they also need to see your idea the same way you see it. They need to see the picture that you are seeing in your mind. No one will put money where their convictions are not. Shiv Khera once said in his book that *"Selling is 90% convincing and 10% persuasion"*. Convincing is about of causing someone to believe that something is true or real. Persuasion means the ability to induce someone to do something through reasoning or argument. All these requires you to say something.

I don't want to take for granted that all of us understand what an 'investor' is, let alone the definition of the term. We might have heard this word more than once at some point in our lives, maybe we have even drawn some conclusions about what the term could possibly mean. I have had the privilege to meet and engage with some of the investors in both Botswana, South Africa, Namibia and some from other continents including Asia and America. I have also had the opportunity to work with some of the investors at our fast growing and yet to be the best entrepreneurship development program in Africa, *The Project124.*

According to the *Oxford dictionary, an investor* is someone who commits capital in order to gain financial returns. That's what an investor is. This is someone, either an individual or an institution who believes so much in your business to an extent that they are even willing to consider risking their own finances to see your business dreams realized. And the key word there is ***risk***. And that's what you need to first understand. Every entrepreneur who decides to open a business needs to understand that the success and/or failure of that business is embedded within their willingness to understand and undertake certain levels of risks. Just because the business makes sense on paper means that it is going to be successful. Have you ever found yourself doing some projections in your calculator and felt like a millionaire? Only to start the thing and see the business taking a different toll. Investors themselves already understand that one to three in every ten of their investments will go big and bring returns.

Now, let's look at it this way, imagine, if someone else out there believes so much in my business that he/she is willing to even risk his/her money on it, surely, I'm telling you, there has to be something about your business that should be compelling him to consider making such decisions. I have been greatly blessed in my life to have one of the first private investors in Botswana as my mentor, Mr. *Arun Iyer*. It's such a great blessing for me to be mentored by him. He is an Indian national but he grew up and amassed his success in business in the land of Botswana. He has dedicated his life towards investing in the development of entrepreneurs across Africa. He taught me a lot about investors and many other different fundamentals relating to funding. It was in the early morning hours when I had visited him at his Alpha Direct offices, and he said to me, *"Goitsemang, if there is something that you need to know and understand is that investors don't come into your business to prove its viability. They don't come to prove the concept. Their duty is to amplify what you are already doing."*, He said as he continued, *"investors don't come to you to start a fire for you, they have to find your little fire already burning and all that they do is that they pour fuel in the fire to make it bigger"*. I loved this analogy because it gave me a much clearer understanding of this topic.

Investors come to boost your business. This are people coming to partner with you on the business. Arun said this at some point, *"Entrepreneurs don't succeed because they have got all the capital, the connections or the skills to push the business"*. Of course, argumentatively, we can debate the matter to some certain degree, but his point which made a lot of sense to me is that, it is good to have all those three as an entrepreneur. But how many of us are privileged enough to have those at our disposal? Not so many of us. Businesses succeeds faster because there is a lot of money being pumped into it to make more money. But here is the point, when you start off, you may not have all of these things. All that you need to do is to improve your ability to attract all these three, more especially the capital. And that's the keyword right there, ***attract***. If you think like an entrepreneur, this will be the right time to act like a prostitute.

You need to ***seduce*** the heart of whoever have got the capital that you need for your business to grow. And the only catch here is that you have got only your words to do the attraction. In other words, you have to find a way to have a conversation with the investors to discuss the deal. There is something called a *pitch* or a *business pitch* if you may prefer it. The word in simple basic elementary English means the shortest form of presentation made by the proposer to the person listening the proposition with the aim of getting a buy-in from that person. The pitch is delivered in so many occasions to different groups of people. Either clients, investors or even business partners.

Neil Patel has once released a very good eye opening article that I believe without a shadow of a doubt that it will change your life. He shared with us some tips on how to deliver a pitch to investors that they can't simply turn down. It takes more than just a will to impress the clients or investors with your pitch. It takes a science. You need to learn from other entrepreneurs who are good with it.

The main thing that you need to understand is that your objective of pitching is not just to get the applause but to sell and advance your vision. The idea here is for you to win the hearts of everybody who will ever come across your idea. The reason why you believe so much in your idea or your business is because there is a picture inside your imagination that gets you up every night you think about it. You need to baptize more people with your dream that it keeps them awake as well. That they see a better world in the future when they get to think about it. You can do this, you just have to learn how to do it. Let me take you through some steps on how to get closer to mastering this simple but complex science that upgraded a lot of entrepreneurs around the world to run globally competitive and wealthy impactful business ventures.

Do this;

First and foremost, ***know your product, your customers and your investor***. You need to be very sure about your story whenever you are talking to anyone about your business, more especially the investors. Investors hears thousands of ideas almost every single month in their lives. It may be your first time to pitch but you should remember that you could be their ten thousand and something pitch to hear in that same period. There's nothing more attractive than seeing someone who is very sure, confident and also competent about what they are talking about. You need take time and study your product. You need to study your customers.

You also need to study your investors that you will be pitching to. Arun taught me that every investor invests on what resonates with their passion. For example, Arun loves 'Fintec' stuff. Finance and technology. If you bring him maybe a horticulture business or a fashion business which don't incorporate 'Fintec' anywhere, chances are that he is automatically going to not be impressed despite how great the pitch was like. You need to know your investors. The most important thing to do when going to war is not to carry the weapons, it is to study the enemy. Investors want to put more than money in your business, they want to also put themselves up in the business to add more value to the business. Well, of course there is a dormant type of investors, but right now we are focusing on venture capitalists whose interest is in seeing you grow into a much bigger business through engaging themselves to see that growth manifesting. People who wants to put their hands to the plough to help you achieve more with their resources at your disposal.

Look, most investors when they listen to a pitch, establishing whether or not someone has a good business idea is the easy part for them to do. By just listening to the content and the structure of your pitch. Most investors walk away because they're not really convinced that they can trust you with their money. It's really that simple. If I don't tell you this, I will have done you an injustice. It's nothing to be angry or bitter about. Think about someone who approaches you and they want to propose to you to spend the rest of your life with them and they don't really sound sure about what they are talking about, more especially when you are a woman. To some, it's a definite **BIG BOLDED NO**. The guy may be very serious about what he is saying, but the fact that what the girl is hearing from his mouth is deficient of some things, it's a total turn off that may even cost him a lot in the long run. You need to study how your customers and your potential investors think. You need to learn what they are passionate about. Know what they will always rather prefer. Know their taste.

Here's a summary of some of Neil Patel's pitching tips which I will try in as much as I can to expand them further for you in the most simplest way I possibly can.

1) Take only ten minutes;

Some people can talk. Like really talk. Given the chance they can talk all day. I'm not saying it is a bad thing. But look, investors are people who often times don't have the luxury of time to commit to one thing, more especially when they had to go out of their way to do it. Giving you a few minutes to hear what you have to say may be the least they can do to show their interest in hearing you out. Say for example you are in a mall somewhere and you bump into one of those people who can invest in your business or help you in any way and they are rushing somewhere, but you have only two minutes to say whatever you have to say to make them interested in hearing more of your idea. The idea is to say a lot by saying a little. Doing more with less. Learn how to pitch in exactly ten minutes. Now, ten minutes is not the standard. There are instances where the pitches can be timed to five minutes, or three minutes, or even just sixty seconds. Whatever shortest time you are given, be ready to deliver on it. The lesser time you take to impress the investor, the better. Practice pitching in the shortest time possible as many times as you can. You will get better at it with time.

2) Turn your pitch into a story;

People love stories, more especially when they touch the spot. It makes them pause a little bit and reflect on their lives. It is more beautiful when they can relate to that story. It becomes personal to them. Everyone has that soft spot in them. There is some story somewhere which can roll a tear down your cheek or put a smile in your face. Now, remember how you came to having that idea. You noticed something. You spotted a gap. Probably via experience or maybe you have witnessed something that either disturbed or infuriated you and you decided to provide a solution to meet that need. Part of the reason why your idea inspires you that much is because there is a story that you know that inspired you to launch your idea. The best thing you would want to do is to share the same story, polished nicely to suit the audience. Always tell a story. Stories knows how to capture imagination better. Once you have captured the imagination, you have captured the person. Remember the idea is for whoever is listening to your pitch to see your idea the same way you see it in your imagination? This is best way to make them see in their imagination what you see in yours. Turn your pitch into a story.

3) Be laser-focused

When given the opportunity to pitch, shoot straight to the point. Remember, you have the time factor governing your pitch. You don't have the luxury of the time to be talking about anything else. Not everything is important. The idea is to share the right and the relevant things. Even in telling the story, you need to find a way of shooting straight to the point without diluting the essence and the sensation of the story. Even when sharing about the idea itself, remember, don't beat around the bush, shoot straight to the point and stay at it.

4) Explain EXACTLY what your product or service is.

This is the most important part of the pitch. Literally. It is what the bride is to the wedding. It is that important. After creating that powerful and sensational introduction of your pitch with your story, you need to find a way in which the story creates a smooth transition that will flow nicely into this part where you are talking about the idea itself. The solution to the problem which the story is trying to paint to the audience. But still again, you need to maintain your focus on shooting straight to the point whenever you talk about something. The word *'explain'* means to give further detailed information on the subject tabled for discussion. It is senior to the word *'define'*. Remember, you are introducing a new concept to somebody else. They need to know what you know about your idea. If it is a product or a service, they need to know what it is. This is exactly why you are pitching, to tell the people about your idea. How does it work? What does it do? How does it do it? Now, of course, a lot of people are not comfortable with sharing some of this information these days. Many have done so and got their hands burnt. Well, it is sad. People are afraid that their ideas may get stolen after they have spilled all the beans to the people. But let us be a little bit more honest and open about this, the purpose of you pitching is because you want someone to entrust you with their money for you to use it to expand your business or bring it into existence. Whatever the case is. But in the end, you want that person to entrust you with that sum of their money to pursue your business.

Now, let me ask you, if you were to entrust me with your money which I am planning on using as my capital to start my business, how much information would you require from me? And what type of information would that be? Exactly, no one will put their money on something they don't trust. And I doubt there is a normal person out there who can trust something they don't know. Of course, there are precautions which I advise you that you take before you will your beans to the people. This is a wicked yet blessed world that we live in. Consult with the intellectual property office in your country about your idea and find out if it is a patentable idea and proceed with the patent if it can be patented. There is a movie I like recommending when talking about this issue, it is called *Syrup*. Find some time and watch it. But don't forget, when pitching, explain exactly what your product or service is. Shoot straight to the point. And say it like someone who knows what they are talking about.

5) Explain exactly what is unique about your product or service.

"If you are not producing or providing anything different from the run-of-the-mill widget, don't even go to the meeting. Go back to your drawing board, and design something better."

- Dr. Strive Masiyiwa

The world is moving forward, not backwards. Every day, the intention is to improve on what we already have. It is a reality, things are not the way they should be. They can always get better. When you create a business, product or service, more especially in this dispensation, you need to be creating something that is better that the world already have. Entrepreneurship in our generation is about giving the world a new experience they have never had. And that's what you need to explain every time you are pitching. How different is your idea from the rest? Let that line of delineation be very visible to the investors when you are pitching.

Even in the case where you are pitching to customers, the truth is, you are going to get this question a lot of times, and *"how different are you from the rest?"* You are entering a market which already has people servicing it. That's what you need to keep in mind. The people are already used to those guys. There is a quote that I was trying to avoid sharing because it took me a little bit longer to understand what it meant, I heard it from one of the guys who joined the first round of the *Project124* when it was launched for the first time in South Africa, it might even take you less time to get it, his name is *Emmanuel Nyahuma.*

Here is the quote;

"I've come up with a set of rules that describe our reactions to technologies:

1. Anything that is in the world when you're born is normal and ordinary and is just a natural part of the way the world works.

2. Anything that's invented between when you're fifteen and thirty-five is new and exciting and revolutionary and you can probably get a career in it.

3. Anything invented after you're thirty-five is against the natural order of things."

— Douglas Adams, The Salmon of Doubt

With this being the reactions of people to "new" things that enters the market, looking at your target market, you need to see how you can best structure your pitch to suit the taste buds of whoever you are pitching to.

6) Explain exactly who your target audience is.

A lot of entrepreneurs struggles to pinpoint to the detail who their target market really is. Entrepreneurship is like hunting, in order to shoot and kill something to eat, you need to know exactly what you are hunting. Use demographic and psychographic features to pinpoint your customers. Show investors a picture of a customer along with relevant data points.

7) Explain exactly how you intend to acquire these customers.

"Business success comes down to marketing. If you have a marketing idea, method, technique or process, this is your chance to showcase it. Contrary to pithy maxims, great products don't sell themselves. You sell the product. To be persuaded, investors have to see an airtight strategy for getting the product to market."

- Dr. Strive Masiyiwa

Most VCs are well aware of the advantages of digital marketing and won't take a second glance at a product that isn't backed by a tactical plan for online marketing.

8) Explain your revenue model.

Investors invest because they want to make a return on that investment. When an investor is listening to you, he/she is only asking themselves about how your company will make them rich. That's it. Do yourself a favor, not only for investors, but for your own benefit as well. Outline your revenue model. Specifically identify which type of revenue model you are embracing, and how you intend to apply it. What exactly makes money in your business?

In his own words the great Strive Masiyiwa, one of Africa's top entrepreneurs, advising young upcoming entrepreneurs he said,

"When you do your pitch, you must remember that; investors are not donors. Investors are not tourists. Investors are not philanthropists or charities. Investors have options. If you have the opportunity to pitch to an investor, consider it a privilege rather than an entitlement:

A good investor will never put money into a venture run by someone who comes across as arrogant, cocky or argumentative.

A good investor will never put money behind someone who is dishonest, corrupt, or a thief. If you have a tendency for dishonesty or misuse of other people's money, a good investor will find out before they give you a cent.

A good investor will not put money behind someone who is careless or disorganized.

A good investor will not invest in someone who is highly emotional. Being passionate is one thing, but being emotional is not acceptable!

A good investor will not invest in someone who is political. You should understand the politics of your country from an economic perspective, but not come across as an active participant in politics.

Being a good investor is very hard. Your job is to show them that you can be trusted with someone else's money."

Investors are and will always be interested in only three things;

Corporate governance: Corporate governance is the system of rules, practices and processes by which a company is directed and controlled. Corporate governance essentially involves balancing the interests of a company's many stakeholders, such as shareholders, management, customers, suppliers, financiers, government and the community.

Accountability: The obligation of an individual or organization to account for its activities, accept responsibility for them, and to disclose the results in a transparent manner. It also includes the responsibility for money or other entrusted property.

Profitability: The state or condition of yielding a financial profit or gain. It is often measured by price to earnings ratio.

CHAPTER 16

LEARN TO NEGOTIATE

"In business as in life, you don't get what you deserve you get what you negotiate"

-Chester L. Karrass

Look, you are not always going to have the things you need for your business to move forward. And most of the time you will not be having the money to acquire those things. I believe that's the beauty of entrepreneurship that makes it even more fun and adventurous. There are times when you are going to get tenders you don't have capital to finance. You are going to get ideas to launch but without capital to pursue them. You are going to get some offers to join certain business investment. Good opportunities has their own ways of coming at the times we least expected and when they come they always find us financially unprepared. This has always been the critical moment that had set apart great entrepreneurs from those that aren't. It is in this moment that the destinies of many great entrepreneurs were birthed. It has been the crossroads for many successful entrepreneurs that we celebrate today. We have always heard about people who built billion dollar portfolios on real estate without not even a single penny that belonged to them in the start. We heard about a lot of many entrepreneurs who are currently seating on a couple of millions and billions of bucks today but started with literally nothing of their own. Life will always give you an opportunity to decide on how big you want to go in life. Many opportunities will come your way and I can guarantee you that they will find you at the time when you have nothing to back you.

Opportunities with latent potential to turn you into a multi-billionaire in a few years will come to you at times when you can't even rub two coins of your own together. But here is something, does the fact that you don't have the capital or access to capital mean you should quit the deal? You may not have the capital, but let me tell you something, you have something that God has graciously given to you which has the same power money has. I'm telling you, this can get you all that you may need to get you to the summit of your success. Do you know what it is? That's your mouth. Not only its ability to affirm positivity to yourself, but its ability to negotiate deals with different people to get things moving in your business. In life, if you don't have money, at least have the ability to negotiate. Two things in the world makes resources exchange hands, that's money and wisdom. Your wisdom, processed in your head and conveyed through your mouth can take you places you never thought you will get. It is the Bible that records that *"the gift of a man shall make a room for him and present him before great men"* There are millions of successful entrepreneurs around the world who only negotiated their way to the top. You can join the army today and negotiate your way to the top. Invest in books like *The Art of the Deal* by *Donald Trump* and improve your skills of negotiation.

When I was a little boy I heard about a story which I don't know how true it is, but I love the wisdom around it. I would probably keep referring to it more than once in other chapters of this book. A story is told that a certain poor old gentleman had a son who was just seating home doing nothing. One day this old man thought to himself and asked himself, *"What can I do to leave a good wealth for my son"*. He rose up from where he was and embarked on a journey to a house of a certain rich man. When he got there he said to the rich man, *"I want my son to marry your daughter"*. The rich man looked at the old man and said to him, *"I don't know if that's going to be possible, what's your son's profile? What does he do?"* The old man replied immediately, *"he seats at home and helps in the house, he didn't complete his school and he can't get a job"*. The rich man looked at the old man and said to him, *"that's not going to be possible Sir, unless maybe your son was at least the chief executive officer of the World Bank"*. The old man's dreams began to seem impossible before his eyes. He went home, when he got home he sat down alone under a tree thinking. As he was thinking, he got an idea. He jumped up and got on the road again, this time he headed straight to the World Bank. When he got there he said to them, *"I want my son to be your chief executive officer"*. They looked at each other in shock. They asked him, *"we hear you old man, but if you don't mind, why do you want your son to be our CEO? What does he have?"* The old man smiled and looked at them and said, *"He is the fiancé to the daughter of the richest man in the world"*. The story teller tells us that the following week after the old man went back to the rich man, the son of the old man was the chief executive officer of the World Bank and also the fiancé to the daughter of the richest man in the world.

Thinking deeper to contemplate on the possibility of this story being true may lead us nowhere, but if we were to take it as it is told, just like I did when I first he it, we may learn a few things that may help us in sharpening our negotiation skills. For us to understand negotiation, we need to first understand that negotiation is not a debate. Although it is a deliberation by two or more parties with varying opinions, the purpose of negotiation is not about winning a motion but an act of sharing thoughts which are orchestrated towards creating a win-win situation for both parties in the deliberation. You need to be able to deliberate and put words across the table that makes the other party comfortable and sold out to the proposition you have tabled to them. In as much as the ability to negotiate is a gift to some, it is also a skill that can be learned. I believe that you can put more effort in acquiring this skill. You need to learn how to make every situation to work in your favor. You can do it. A lot of entrepreneurs have saved their companies a lot of money as well as acquired their companies a lot of resources to do projects bigger than them by investing in their ability to negotiate. I highly recommend that you consider doing it as well.

Here is some tips on where to start in improving your negotiation skills; learn to be confident. It takes time, but do it anyway. Do your homework. Understand the value that the person you are negotiating with has put on the outcomes of the negotiation. Learn the person you are negotiating with. Define your goals. Know what you want in the deal. I think one of the problems that we have more especially here in Botswana is that many people are afraid to be open and honest about what they want from the deal. We always want to leave it to assumptions. You get into a deal, you don't disclose your expectations to the other party that for instance, you want to make money out of the deal. And how much are you expecting to benefit from the deal. I have dealt with many cases where business partners started a business together for so many years, but they never opened a conversation amongst themselves to talk about their equity shareholding. They both know that they have equity in the business, but they never discussed how much equity each partner owns. It is like when you are taking a walk with your friend and it happens that your friend finds a hundred dollar bill on the ground by the side of the road, by the time your friend picks it up, without negotiation or any form of conversation, you automatically feel that you own 50% of that money. And you expect your partner to give you that share. What happens when your friend decides to give you 10% of the money? Or nothing at all? I know you will feel cheated, but what is the basis of your argument? Why do you think you deserve 50% of the money?

My point is, even when it comes to starting businesses with partners, most partners allocate their equity in that manner. Just because you start a business with someone doesn't mean they automatically own 50% share of the business. Everyone's contribution to the company must be valued and allocated proper share. As an entrepreneur, you must have a thick skin to stand your ground when you negotiate. You must gather your facts together. You must know your numbers. Negotiation is not an emotional conversation, it is a logical and rational conversation. I have personally had my ups and downs when I was growing my negotiation skills. When I was doing my first year at university, I met one guy from another university. He was selling accounting and business management textbooks. The books were very cheap, it was P250 per book. I felt like if I could sell them at my own school, I could make a lot of money. The problem was that I didn't have money to buy the books from this guy to resell them at my school. We agreed with the guy that I will bring customers to him and he will give me commission.

I brought the first 5 customers, the guy paid me P25 (P5 per customer). But he made P1'250 in this sale. I was furious. But then again, coming to think about it later, I asked myself, how much was he supposed paid me? We didn't agree on how much the commission was. I just thought that he will be human enough to give me something significant knowing that I'm bringing good business to him. I never even investigated where this guy gets the books where he can afford to sell them at this low prices. I only found out later that he was also a middleman. He has a guy who is buying the books with his student card from the university book store using his free credits. And he was giving him 35% commission per book sale. So I was technically bringing business to this guy for him to transact without having to work not even a day while I was getting peanuts from the deal. Mark Cuban once said *"Always look for the fool in the deal, if you don't find one, it's you"*.

Do your job, learn to be the best negotiator.

CHAPTER 17

SCRATCH THE ITCH

"A satisfied customer is the best business strategy of all"

-Michael LeBoeuf

For years now, the world has been holding conversations about *disruption*. I want to take this moment and seat on this for a while. I think it is very important for us to realize that we live in a world that changes every single week. Things change. As entrepreneurs our main goal is add value to how our customers live their day to day life as they interact with the world on daily basis. We need to be cognitive to the fact that their needs changes every now and then. Of course, we were taught growing up about customer loyalty, but welcome to the world where none of that matters anymore. Relevance is everything.

In today's world of entrepreneurship, unless and until we as entrepreneurs can be able to create products or services that can save our customers time, energy, resources or all the above, we will not make the cut. In this world of increasingly growing competition and change in the markets, we have to be determined as African entrepreneurs to create businesses that will offer great value cheaper, better and faster to our customers. If we are not up to the task, entrepreneurs from the rest of the world will do so and what we have seen happening to many companies before in different continents we will see happening right here in Africa with us as victims.

I am fully convinced that we as African entrepreneurs are well and able to scratch the itch of big markets around the world. McDonalds for years has maintained a growing huge market share in the fast foods business because of their business model that served the customers with a full hamburger meal within an incredible short period of time. Because of their focus on the speed of delivery and not the food itself, a big door opened for a new comer. Shake Shack got into the picture.

It has to be noted that Shake Shack started as a very simple hamburger stand but capitalized in what the big rival took for granted for many years. With an increasing awareness for proper eating and health management because of the many reports headlining every day about people dying every single day due to unhealthy foods, many people today value what they eat more than how fast they can get to eat it, although speed is still a very crucial factor in the equation. Danny Meyer found a niche to grow Shake Shack business in the direction of offering healthy hamburgers and shakes as fast as they can with a variety of options available for customers to make a choice that suits them better. The emphasis now has shifted from 'fast' to 'food'.

Now, let's just say all prostitutes around the world somehow meet and reach a consensus and just declare that for the next six months or so their doors will be closed. What impact will that move bring? In fact, six months is a lot of time. Let's say six weeks, even six days. A lot of entrepreneurs have a tendency of starting and operating businesses which its business models are not built on the frameworks of meeting a certain need. There are thousands and possibly millions of entrepreneurs around whose businesses are prospering simply because they are serving the market with products and services which the clients can't live without.

Our greatest struggle in entrepreneurship more especially for us start-ups is building a growing clientele base. Most of the time you will find out that our problem is not in generating leads but converting the leads into customers then to clients. One thing that we need to understand as entrepreneurs is that people should not buy our products and services out of pity. They should not buy our products because they know us. Look, hear me very well. It is okay to get support from your close people more especially when you are a start-up. In fact, entrepreneurs needs that for them to keep pushing. It means a lot to do something with the knowledge that there are people somewhere backing your grind up.

If we could take time and read biographies of many great entrepreneurs that inspires many of us today we will surely find somewhere where they wrote about how getting support from their families played a huge role in their success. I'm not disputing that. But we need to understand that if we are to build globally competitive business ventures we cannot afford to base our sales on pity. People should not buy our products and services just because they pity us. They should buy them because they add value to their lives. Just because it sounds like a great idea to you means that the market will accept it. I've met so many aspiring entrepreneurs before and listened to them as they began to pitch their ideas to me. You could tell by the smiles in their face while they are talking about their ideas that they are so convinced that it's a great idea that's going to change the world. The moment I ask them the question that I ask every entrepreneur during pitches; *"so, what is the market saying about this product?"* Surprising as it may be, many entrepreneurs get into business without first carrying out at least a basic feasibility study. Many entrepreneurs just think that just because it sounds like a great idea (to them) that's all they need to start.

There are so many factors that every entrepreneur needs to know which determines the success of any thing that is regarded as a business. In these book we will just consider a few which are highly imperative. As we have already talked about it earlier, it very important for you as an entrepreneur to employ proper preparation on your entrepreneurial journey. I'm not saying go to school and learn about how to start a business (which is also recommended), but you can also just continue reading this book, I believe by the time you are halfway way through the book you will be close to being almost knowledgeable about a few things about business and entrepreneurship pending your practice for you to be an en expert. I believe your business pedigree and repertoire will improve as this book continues.

One thing that you need to keep in mind is that no one was born an expert. It took discipline to gather few doses of knowledge and wisdom from different people here and there and built the revelation knowledge that they do possess today. Whenever you read a book, you are actually absorbing someone's experience into yourself in a very short time. If you read Robert Kiyosaki's books, you are taking into your system what took him a lot of years to learn the hard way through trial and error to become an expert in just the few hours you spent reading that book. I believe that as you read this book together with other books by other great people in line with your industry or purpose you will soon possess tones of knowledge that will pay back sooner than you think. I tell people all the time that the difference between competitors is simply the knowledge each one of them possess. The other one is beating the other simply because he knows something his/her competitors doesn't know. It's funny when you get to learn that your competitor's competitive edge is sponsored by the books you have in your shelf you have not read. And again, one of my great mentors, Boago Ramogapi once made a statement during his talk at a seminar I attended, he said, *"it is not what you hear that matters, but it is what you do with what you hear that matters the most"*. Don't just know, act on what you know.

If your target market is other businesses (business to business trading), your business should focus either on making your customers money or saving them money. If your target market is people, then your focus should be on creating the best value for their money. Always keep this in mind that if there is another product somewhere with great value and selling at a price slightly lower than your price, customers will always buy that product. Look, you may say that you are an entrepreneur and all, but I believe that every entrepreneur is a customer somewhere. Let's look at it from that perspective. There are some places where you really enjoy shopping at. You don't buy there because you support their business, you buy there because there is an itch in you that their products or services are scratching for you. And you keep back again. This business has now become part of your life.

Well, for me, I can admit to a few businesses, shops and products I find myself intertwined with. But there are businesses, products or services that it does matter how bad life is, regardless of whether Justin Bieber said *"never say never"* or not, you will never buy from them. The world is getting smarter every day. Financial literacy is growing in the world daily. Gone are the days where most entrepreneurs were capitalizing on the ignorance of people to generate more profits. Your customers are not stuck with you.

By just a simple click of a button, you may lose your market to another business which is more committed to meeting the needs of the people at the most affordable prices possible. The people are not only concerned about the price of the sale, they are also concerned about the cost of this sale. The market is already weeping due to their income related issues. The minimum wages are either going down or constant. The cost of living is escalating every day. Job retrenchments are taking place almost everywhere in the world. There is so much unemployment. The market is looking for products or services that will help them mitigate all these challenges that they are faced with on daily basis. You can't target the middle income group and create products for them that costs more than 40% of their monthly income. Today' business is not only about generating profits, it is about sharing in the problems and challenges that are affecting your target market and embark into offering them a flexible access to your products and services. We have to help our customers to buy from us.

I personally love how *Elon Musk* has modelled his *Tesla* business. To me, this is a true semblance of a visionary who sees and seeks to make life much simpler for many people to enjoy it. His decision to make an electric car, starting with the fact that in their statement they said *"we want to make every car in the road electric"*. By thinking beyond the norm and revolutionizing the motor industry through the introduction of the electricity powered cars that moves without even a single drop of fuel, this will mean that carbon dioxide emissions are dropped drastically which will add value to the lives of people living on earth. What I loved more than everything else is that Elon Musk through Tesla created a car that will have the same experience of sexiness, luxurious driving and long distance coverage just like the other expensive cars (most people can't afford to buy) do but he created it with margins that could allow him to offer it to the market for a small fraction of what the other expensive cars cost. As he was launching the Model S, over 20'000 people had believed enough in his vision that they pre-ordered the car as it was just offered for as little as $15'000 apiece.

Aspire to be relevant. Commit to continuously develop your solution. Persist long enough to always carry your dream to another level. The people will always stick to the businesses that makes their lives simpler and meaningful. You need to define yourself clearly to the market. Build your brand so good that it can be remembered by many people for just one simple keyword. Let people trust you for what you offer. Satisfy people's needs so great that they volunteer to refer many people to you with all the confidence in the world.

CHAPTER 18

GETTING YOUR BUSINESS TO THE PEOPLE

"We determine who we are by what we do"

- Hitman

If we were to focus on the truth and the truth only, we will find out that the success and failures of many businesses out there can be traced back to one thing; *proper marketing*. Most of the time people limit marketing to the process of getting people to be aware of a certain business, product or service. Marketing is beyond that. As we have already discussed in other chapters of this book, it is highly important for you as an entrepreneur to know exactly what it is that you want to offer the Business world. Far and beyond that, there's a few other things that you might need to learn too. Your business cannot be profitable unless and until the market is consuming its products or services. Look, you can create the best product in the world, but unless and until you take it up in the market, your business will never be profitable. But before you consider doing so, because I subscribe to the philosophy that says *"if you are to do it, don't just do it, always try to do it the better way",* I believe that there is the better way of going about this. The following are a few guides on how to do it better for your company;

1) Target the right people

First and foremost, you need to be able to define your target market. I normally hear people saying *"my product will be targeting young people*". I will tell you the truth, it won't sound wrong until you go out there and try to find young people to sell to. When you don't know who your real target market is, chances are that you are just shooting in the dark hoping to make a killing, and chances are that you are not making any killing at all while experiencing real losses.

Metaphorically speaking, think of this, when designing a dress, what do you think are the key things that you need to know before designing the dress? You cannot design a suitable dress if you don't know who you are designing it for. Because you don't know who you are designing it for chances are that you don't know the size of the dress you should design. Because you don't know the size of the dress you should design you won't know the quantity of the cloth/material you need to design the dress. You may know the patterns you would love to design, but minus the real customer in the picture, more especially when you are a start-up business and you are looking forward to grow in the business, or maybe you have gotten a loan to do the business, it's quite suicidal to do business that way.

You need to know your real target market. Don't generalize. Specify. When you have specified your target customer, it will be easier for you to know the size of this target market. It makes it easier for you to quantify it. It actually gives you a more realistic view of your target market. It will also help you to know the location of your target market. When you know the location of your target market then you will be able to find the proper way of getting your business to them. Both raising the awareness of your product/service to distributing it to your target. You see? Different components that will result in your business success will keep on unfolding. When you know the location, the distance, the accessibility of your target market, then you will be able to know the mediums you can employ to reach your target market.

You don't just print flyers because people print flyers. You don't just open stores because people open stores. You do what you do because that's what matters necessitates. Do it because that's what reaches your target market and delivers your pro and services to your target market. Don't be afraid to be creative with it. Know your position in the market. Know the numbers by head. This is what your potential investors wish you would have done by the time you come to them. They don't want vague and unrealistic opinion on the market, they need the realistic size of your market because that's the only number they can multiply with your selling price to get their potential profits. In a nutshell, know where you stand in the market.

Just because somebody needs your products or services means they are automatically your target market. I will tell you the truth, in my coaching experience and many other businesses I have tried in the past, I've had bad experience with targeting the *'wrong right people'*. I will repeat this that just because somebody needs your products or services means that they are automatically your target market. You don't need people who only need your products or services, you need people who need your products or services and they have the money to pay for them. Even as we speak, I have done so many jobs for so many people who needed services from me, and what's painful is that I had budgeted for that money as my working capital for a few months I was busy doing the job, but even as we speak right now those people still can't pay me.

Most of us new entrepreneurs we like having mercy on our clients and feeling sorry for them when we do business with them. I remember my last day at my first office, I was seating in my office chair and wondering, I had just received my eviction notice themed *'please evacuate the office with immediate effect',* I asked myself, "why is it that I can have mercy on my clients when they can't pay me but my landlord can't have mercy on me as his client when I can't pay him". I remembered at that point that those Indian guys (my landlords) was running a company, and not a charitable organization, and so did I. From that point I made a decision that I will do business the way business should be done. And that's firstly targeting the right people. The customer is the right one when they need your products or services, and more importantly, that customer able to pay for those products or services. Have peace with the fact that you are going to start saying no to helping people who can't pay. Unless your business is a charity.

2) Learn your people

Learn the people, not just people, but learn your people, because when you have learnt your people you will know their problems. When you know their problems that's when you will know how to best help them. The moment they see your business as the solution to their problems, and they are willing to exchange value for it, you are in business. If you will be good in that provision of the solution, you will be in business for the longest time. Learn your customer behaviors. Learn their preferences. Learn their habits. Learn about their belief systems. Only when you know and understand your people can you serve them better.

It's like in relationships, the best way to love your partner better is by learning who your partner really is. We don't love our partners according to how we prefer to love them, we love them according to how they would love to be loved. Relationships are more about how you make your partner feels about herself/himself more than how you feel about them. The inverse is also true. And the only way to love your partner in the way that they will see a future with you is by first learning your partner. Similarly, business is also about relationships. Relationships with your clients. Relationships with your employees. Relationships with your partners. Relationships with your suppliers. Relationships with your investors. Relationships with your authorities. As entrepreneurs, we need to invest in learning about our people. All the people that makes our businesses what they are. The future of our businesses depends on the quality of the relationships we have with all our people. Only mutual understanding can get two people far in what they are doing. There's nothing that beats the good relationship between entrepreneurs and their clients. Always strive to have that great relationship with yours, including all the other people in your business network.

3) Understand the power of great business

Business is about relationships. A great business is the business that's able to serve a client so perfectly that the client keeps coming back for more with more other people. That's the business that we want. That's the business that we should have. That's the business level that we should work toward getting our businesses towards. Imagine a well-oiled business machine putting smiles in the face of many people as well as on your business bank account. When you have positioned yourself well and you have learned your business, you stand a very good chance of improving your delivery mastery that will make your business a great business.

One other thing that you probably need to learn is turning people's wants into needs. In today's highly competitive business world, many businesses survives through their radical marketing campaigns formulated to retain and grow their customer base by turning people's wants into needs. They learnt how to take advantage of the trends in the society and channel their business in that direction to generate more profits. We are Africans, well, some of us, and to every African country that I have ever been to, every parking lot has these guys who have made it a hobby to help people park their cars. They have made huge profits out of it. Look, they didn't build parking lots. They didn't teach people how to drive. They didn't even go to school to train themselves on how to drive and park cars. All they did is that they saw an opportunity to help many people to find open parking spaces and helped them to park in those spaces nicely. The service is optional, but many people have turned this service into a need. Find parking spaces is a difficult thing to do in a city, crime rates have gone high. This is why many drivers believe so much that this service shouldn't be considered a want but a need. As we speak, the state police departments in different cities and countries are partnering with these guys to fight crime in the parking lots.

As we were launching the *Project124* in Johannesburg (South Africa), one of the powerful young South African entrepreneurs, actress and speaker, *Mbali Nngwenya* made a very powerful statement, she said, *"Make your product so good that people will rather compromise on everything else expect your products"*. Imagine. Just imagine yourself in millions and billions of people's budget every single month. You can build your business so good that one (if not all) of its products or services reflects on people's budgets every month. This should be your goal. A business that's there to help people live a better life for long and cheaper. This can be your business.

CHAPTER 19

KEEP THE BUSINESS GOING

"The magic is not in starting a business, the magic is in staying in business"

- *Goitsemang J. Khutsafalo*

The magic is not in starting a business. The magic is in keeping the business going. Look, from my little experience, I can tell you that the most difficult part of entrepreneurship is in maintaining the business growth. Many companies dies during their growth period. Many companies are killed by poorly managed growth. It was easy for you to start the business. In fact, starting, that's where the fun is. Running around doing this and that. Getting calls from people asking about your business. Having approximately ten customers that you are servicing. It's so fun. You feel like a real entrepreneur. I believe every entrepreneur enjoyed this phase of their business. It's like your first day at school. You still hyped up. You feel fired up and ready to go. Getting to meet new people, gain new experiences. You get some recognition here and there. Everything is going well. Then suddenly, the first tire burst and only real drivers can be seen.

A lot of things will happen in your entrepreneurial journey. They are not new. Many other entrepreneurs out there went through them as well. It's a fact. It doesn't matter who you are or where you come from, some disappoints and other very discouraging things are going to come to your attention. They say in life it is either you are in a problem or you just got out of one or you are headed towards one, I believe in business this statement still applies. Entrepreneurship begins with identifying problems to solve, that's how it gets you to own a business, it doesn't end there, and many other challenges are going to affect the very same business which is trying to solve another problem, that's where you as an entrepreneur you need to prove that you are the entrepreneur whom you claim to be. It never ends, from the beginning to the current moment in every business, there is always one job to do; solving problems after problems. Entrepreneurship is like that ancient unicycle, you need to keep balancing yourself to stay on top and to keep moving. If you stop cycling you will definitely fall. You can't move with only one foot on the pedal, you need both feet doing what is required of them at the time they are required. I gave an illustration before during one of my presentations that running a business is like trying to get married to a girl who doesn't want to get married to you, but until you up your game to somewhere, maybe, just maybe, something can happen.

Our efforts in business should only carry either of the two motives all the time;

Maintaining the business

Taking the business to the next level

If whatever you want to do does not fuel this two, don't do it. Never confuse activity for productivity. The bottom line of every business is primarily profits. You are not running a charitable organization, you are running a business venture. How is everything you are doing taking your business forward? Every time you are doing something you are spending something, either your time or your other resources.

I once heard a story somewhere and I would like to share the story with you. The teller of the story began to say, there was a certain man called Caleb. Caleb was hired by the French men who had come to his island and found out that a lot of people have lost their lives in a lot of ship wrecks that took place in that island almost every month. To circumvent the problem, the French men decided to build a fuel based twilight tower on that island and hired Caleb to take care of the tower to ensure that the light on the tower is always on so that when ships approach the island they may see it from afar and not crash on the island. The French man would normally come once a month to this island to bring fuel for the lamp. The fuel was only enough to keep the lights on for a full month. It happened that as Caleb was on duty, every once in a while a certain group of old women would come to the tower and ask for a little fuel to light up their house lamps. He felt pity for them and he would give them some of the fuel to light their lamps. They would come once a week. Today only one of them comes, and tomorrow another one.

It happened that as the last week of the month approached, the light at the tower began to dim. When Caleb went to check the fuel he found out that there was no enough fuel left in the fuel tank. Two days before the French men arrived at the island, the lights switched off. In that very same night, the most disastrous and biggest accident that killed tens and hundreds of people happened. I have personally learnt from this particular narrative that we need to learn to be disciplined when it comes to the management of company resources. Each penny that the company has, have to be put in the right place where it will advance the company's growth. We may take it lightly that we are giving away small amounts of money, or we are spending small amounts money, forgetting that the dams are filled to capacity by a countless drops of water. All these small monies that we don't mind losing in different occasions, all these small amounts of monies that we keep dipping our hands into for our personal use, when put together, companies are bleeding huge amounts of money because of it. We need the discipline to manage our company resources appropriately. When the company's resources are well managed, the company's future is secured.

It is very important that we understand that the day we signed up for entrepreneurship, we signed up for something that should never stop. When Mr Kentucky started KFC back in the days, they needed to understand that it had to keep existing even to date whether Mr. Kentucky dies or not. Of course, it hasn't been our culture in Africa to participate in the business of creating multi-generational businesses. Many of us here, our death will mean that of our businesses, if by any chance they themselves don't die before we do. You need to ask yourself a question that I always ask myself, *"is there going to be a time on earth where the people are going to say, there used to be company-X"*, referring to your company. How long do you want that business of yours to exist? It may take you a while to build a reputable business but trust me, you only need a few seconds to destroy it. I will ask you this, for some of you who are already running some businesses, if you were to continue doing what you are doing daily with your business, where do think it will be in the next ten years? Thirty years? Hundred years? The success of every business will always be traced to its management and administration. Most business did not die because the ideas were poor, they died because they were poorly managed. Even as we speak, there are businesses which are worth a quarter of what they could be worth now if they were managed properly.

I understand that many of us did not have the privilege to go through proper training on how to properly manage a business, but it's okay, we shall discuss a few things which may add good value to your business knowledge and pedigree. I always ask my clients this question which I will ask you right now, *"If you were you were your own competitor, how were you going to kick your own butt?"* It is expedient of you that you understand that you are not only facing pressure coming from the internal demand to keep up with certain standards, you are faced with another pressure coming from your competitors who if they do something better than you it puts you on the verge of losing your clientele. Your client is not your wife who you will always find when you get home every evening, your client is your girlfriend who have other boyfriends out there you don't know about. It's up to her who she checks up on, if you don't have 'that thing', she may go for good and you will never see her. She won't unfriend you on Facebook, you are going to keep seeing her pictures of her and the other new boyfriend captioned *"he completes me"*, days after she has gone silent on you. Of course, there are some who will say it to your face that *"it's over"*. How do you think your barber will feel if he sees you in the mall with a new haircut but he hasn't seen you in a while?

Look, you can't force a client to stay in your business, you can only attract them to your business, and you can only keep them in the business only if you offer them what they can't get out there. Always remember, they have a choice to leave any time they want. Business is about adding value to the clients in exchange for profits. The longevity of your relationship with your clients determines the health of your cash flow, and only your cash flow can determine how long you are going to survive as a company. So keeping the business going is in essence keeping the relationship with your clients going while building new relationships with more clients for expansion and growth purposes. You should know also that there is a huge difference between customers and clients. Customers are those people who buys once and go, maybe never come back. I am sure you have bought something before at a certain shop somewhere and you have never been there ever after that for whatsoever reason. Clients are those people who keep buying from you. You can count on them that they are going to come and buy at a particular interval. Those are the people you want. Those are the people you should be channeling your energies and resources towards building up in your business.

It is not easy to build a proper clientele base. It is something that requires determination. Almost every form of success requires a certain level of determination. You cannot achieve anything in this lifetime without the application of any form of determination. Of course, we are humans. Sometimes our level of determination fluctuates based on our experiences at the time of our efforts to build a clientele base. The truth is, some of us are really trying, but we keep getting frustrated along the way because of some things that we encounter. I am going to take you through a few steps of building and growing your clientele base. This may be for your application or just appreciation. Keep in mind the words of Boago Ramogapi who said that "it is not what we hear that matters but what we do with what we hear that matters the most", I hope you will find the following steps useful.

The mistake that a lot of entrepreneurs and other kinds of business people do is to invest in the knowledge of how to craft the product or service they are to offer the market and forget to invest in the knowledge of how to run a business that offers those products or services. You will find out that in a pharmacy, the doctor is good with mixing the chemicals to create good medicine but he doesn't know how to run a business of creating those medicines. Or a barber good with haircuts and hairdos but he doesn't know how to run a saloon business. But simply because they are the ones who came up with the idea of that business and they are the ones who are doing the actual job, they are automatically the business leadership. As an entrepreneur you should be good with the two, or at least get someone who will be good with the other. But for your appreciation and learning, the next chapter will teach you about the few basic things you should know about running a growing and profitable business. Just five things, they are the ones which determines the life or death of any company.

CHAPTER 20

DO BUSINESS THE PROFITABLE WAY

"Success and profitability are outcomes of focusing on customers and employees, not objectives."

-Jack Ma

The bottom line of doing business is to make profits. Our margins has to be very good. Our expenses has to be as low as possible while our margins are high. A great entrepreneur plus a great business makes the best combination in the world. A great business is a business with a great product, incredible people and great processes. Yes, that's what brings profitability to any business in the world. The 3 P(s) of business; People, process and product. Most entrepreneurs are losing a lot of money every single year because of the poor management of their businesses. Either through the work ethic or competence of the people who are working in the business, or the business processes that the business has decided to use to render the services to the clients. Sometimes businesses loses money through the way they package their own products/services. Considering the quality of the product, the relevance as well as the efficiency of the products, you will find out that businesses are bleeding a lot of money out of the business every year because of their inability to serve the market efficiently, effectively and profitably.

If there is a business that will grow into a successful business, it is a business that will be good with the following;

Leads generation

Conversion

Transactions frequency maximization

Cash flow management

Mastery

Business is about acquiring and keeping customers and clients. That is what it is called *'building a clientele base'*. Why is it that every time somebody asks you saying *"how is business?"* the first thing that comes to your mind is *"performance, clients, and profits"?* Your mind already knows the things that will always matter in the end. It is not about how busy you have been all along, it is your cash flow statement which we are interested in ultimately. Acquiring and keeping clientele, while acquiring more without losing the balance and control of your business. You remember the unicycle illustration we talked about earlier? The idea is for you to learn how to ride a unicycle and having to carry bricks with you without losing the balance and the motion, adding one more brick at a time. Let's get into the above five points we mentioned above. Some of you might have been privileged before to get the opportunity to learn about those things from somewhere else, but for those who are seeing them for the first time, let's take this moment to learn one more crucial thing;

Leads generation

I am fully aware that you have heard of the term 'marketing' before. Right? When I say marketing, what comes to your mind? You might be imagining yourself wearing the uniform or brand of your company somewhere distributing flyers or mounting posters around town. You might be imagining yourself getting house to house and office to office telling people about your business. You might be imagining yourself creating and sponsoring adverts on Facebook and other social media platforms. You could be imagining yourself commenting somewhere in a seminar and chipping in a few words about the business that you do. Maybe you imagined yourself standing in front of your stall somewhere in a shopping Centre and speaking to a crowd of people about your business. Anything that you could have imagined yourself doing, that's okay, we can work with that. Let me tell you the truth, there are companies which regards marketing as an expense and those that regards marketing as an investment. It costs a few bucks, and sometimes a lot more to design and print flyers, posters and banners. It costs a certain amount of bucks to do any form of marketing. Sometimes these are the monies that we don't have. I have seen different companies putting in thousands of bucks as their budget for marketing and coming out with nothing.

Have you ever got a flyer from someone before in a mall who was trying to market himself/herself to you and you didn't even bother to look at it and just went and throw it into the next bin you could find? Sometimes five meters away from where he/she was standing. Did you know that eight in ten people who are given a flyer in the mall and other places do that all the time? Well, the statistics may not be that accurate but that cannot discount nor discredit the fact that a huge chunk of people receiving flyers our there considers them a waste of time regardless of what's written in them. If that's what you do to other entrepreneurs out there during their marketing endeavor, what makes you think that others won't do the same to you on your own marketing endeavors? I am not in any way saying you should stop printing and distrusting flyers. This is what I am saying. When you get into business, one of the most important things after identifying the product or service you want to offer the market, you need to define your target market. You need to be able to quantify your market. You need to be able to describe your target market even to the smallest detail. Who is your customer, where are they? How many are they? You will be surprised that there are entrepreneurs out there who have businesses and they have no idea who they are targeting. One of the mistakes I have done when I got into business was targeting the wrong customers simply because I thought they were the right people for my services. The truth is, they looked like my target audience. They needed my services, but the problem was that they could not afford even the hugely discounted prices that I offered them. I have seen a lot of businesses failing because they got all their initial stock locked up by people by people who can't pay for. More especially small stock businesses which a lot of people are going for these days.

The truth is, your business cannot survive without clients and customers. To get customers, it is not just about doing marketing, it is about doing it right. Knowing what you are doing and having it working for your business. Most of the things that we are doing in our entrepreneurship journey we are just doing them because we have copied them from other people and pasting it in our businesses without even considering the reason why those people whom we copied from applied the same thing in their businesses in the first place. Of course, I agree, we have to learn from each other and improve ourselves, but it is wise also for you to do the things you do in your business with understanding.

It is very important to understand to the core that we are serving different types of customers and clients. Different customers needs different types of lead generation methods. Identifying your target market helps you to understand the strategies you need to employ in order to fish those customers. Marketing is beyond making noise about your business and creating brand awareness (which is what many of us love doing), it is about having the same people who are aware of our products and services show up at our companies to bring business to us.

Lead generation is about making more people interested in your products or services. That's it. Say, you have recently developed a crush on someone and he/she seems to not be aware of it. You see them all the time, but still, it's like you are invisible. Every time they pass by you feel like shouting *"hello? Hi, are you blind?"* Ladies will understand this better. It hurts, like really hurts for ladies to take all the time on earth to seat in front of the mirror, put on her best make-up, put on her best dress, polish her nails, do her hair, only to come back without at least single compliment. Imagine putting up your best selfie on either Facebook or Instagram and you only get 3 likes from the friends of your friends. Do something every day in your business that will make people interested in your business. Go out. Make noise about your business. Whatever you do, make people to want to do business with you.

Conversion

Business is about the numbers. I guess by now you have realized the need for your understanding of these numbers. One of the numbers that you need to ultimately know by head about your company is what it is called *conversion ratio.* A lot of people have tried to teach about this differently in so many occasions, but my understanding of this term, which I believe it will be simpler for you to learn is this, as we have already talked about leads generation, the conversion ratio is interested in knowing and quantitatively state the number of prospects you were able to convert into clients. Let's use this example, say in your marketing campaign you managed to reach 400 people, and of the 400 people, only about 200 of them showed interest in your product, and now, out of the 200 only 70 of them signed up as your clients. What we would then do to find out your conversion ratio is that we will divide the number of the converted clients by the number of prospects and multiply it by 100 to get the percentage value.

Which in our example it will be;

$$70/200 \times 100 = 35\%$$

The conversion rate as this example states will be 35%.

Many businesses don't really know their conversion rate. They don't know how many prospects they get per a given amount of time. They can't really tell you how many people walk through their doors showing interest in their businesses, how many people called asking about the products or services, how many people inboxed their Facebook page asking about the same thing. They don't know how many people e-mailed their company expressing their interest on their products. They have no idea at all. All that they know is that a lot of people shows interest, but they can't quantify it. A lot of businesses miss out on huge profits because of their reluctance when it comes to managing their conversion ratios. You need a higher conversion ratio. Conversion ratio is what will show you if your marketing strategy is worth continuing with it or not. Marketing or leads generation is not one of the activities that businesses can do, it is the major activity which businesses MUST DO. Always. But it should be done with understanding. It should be done with outlined objectives that can be quantified. Marketing is not about throwing money to get your brand across. Marketing is an investment. It is the act of buying your customers to buy in your business. You need to know how much business does each dollar you spend on your marketing brings to your business. You have to capitalize on each prospect that comes across. Look at it as fishing, when you fish and catch a fish with a net, you don't just put it there, you make sure you kill it and keep it safe somewhere. You don't say I will kill it later, otherwise you will find it gone. How many people have long said that you should call them for business? How many people are still waiting for your response on your company's Facebook page? When are you going to respond to those people?

Invest on certain packages specifically designed for new clients. Have some you are offering customers to feel welcome and to look forward to enjoy more of your incentives. It doesn't have to be a big thing. First impressions counts. As you recruit customers through your leads generation activities, have irresistible packages and incentives that will make the customers to want to keep buying from you. Sometimes converting a customer to a client may take a while. Even months. You will be like a guy who is proposing a girl who is still either dating someone else or eyeing someone else. Most customers are already being serviced by other entrepreneurs. Some are being serviced poorly and some are enjoying the great service they are receiving from these entrepreneurs. Others have given up and settled for the poor services they are being given. Most of your prospects will be made up of these different types of customers with different experiences. It's up to you to position yourself to be attractive to them and most importantly, be able to scratch their itch in the manner in which they will be convinced in their hearts that your business is now their new home.

Transaction Frequency & volumes Maximization

The truth is, business is about making money. Over and above adding value to the societies that we exist in, we need to generate value as well in different forms, both financial and non-financial. In everything that we do, the objective should always be about one thing; getting somebody to buy from us. Not only that, to get one more person to buy from us. It is about transactions. It is about how many of those transactions do we get and how we can increase them and how we can get them faster. When we embark in all the marketing and sales activities, we need to know at the back of our mind what we are actually trying to achieve. Mathematically. Let's take an example, there are businesses which receives ten customers a week. And maybe per customer visit they make about a hundred bucks, this means that the company makes a thousand a week, we can then safely say the company make four thousand bucks a month. And if everything remains constant in all the other months, we can also safely say that the company makes about forty eight thousand bucks a year. Depending on who you are, to some this is satisfactory business performance. To some, myself included, this is not good enough. We are different. For some of us who want to go big, for some of us who want to reach dimensions never reached in our generation, for some of us who want to run globally competitive business ventures, there's a push without that we can do better.

I have got to learn that most of these billion dollar businesses didn't become billion dollar businesses by selling billion dollar products. No, most of them became billion dollar businesses by selling a one dollar product to a billion people. Or alternatively, they became billion dollar businesses by selling one dollar products a billion times. Business takes time to be built into a great success story. We need to get to a level where we can see a billion dollar company in the small businesses that we do. I can assure you, a one dollar business with a billion dollar vision will one day become a billion dollar company. The magic is in the company's willingness to invest time and other resources to grow its clientele base from 10 clients to 100 clients. To move it from 100 clients to 1'000 and so forth. By all means possible, you need to see how you are going to grow your company from making a thousand transactions a month to ten thousand transactions. You need to see a way in which you can move your company from making a hundred bucks per customer visit to two hundred bucks per customer visit. There are simple strategies that you can develop for your company to achieve to achieve this goal. It is possible for you to double and even triple your company's revenues by developing and deploying these strategies into your business. Learn to manage your company like somebody who is competing at a global scale.

Customers have a way of reducing you to the product or service that they bought from you. That's why they even saved your number on their phones with the name of the product that they bought from you. *"Cake lady"*. *"Logos Guy"*. *"Shoe maker"*. *"Electrician guy"*. Etc. Do you know why? Because that's what they know you to be. That's what they know you can help them with. But here is the thing, did you know that some of your customers buys some of the products that you are selling elsewhere? Sometimes even from your competitors? The truth is, most of them do so because they didn't know that you also offer those products or services. You will be surprised to know how most of your customers will be surprised to hear that you have more to offer them for a very good price. You have to ensure that as a company you position yourself in a way in which your customers are aware of everything that you offer. When you get to these big restaurants, whenever you order a meal, the cashiers will always ask you if you will be interested in some of their new products and meals. You may be buying your favorite meal from that restaurant, but they will always introduce you to other meals you may have never considered.

When you walk into retail stores and mega department stores, you will always find sweets, chocolates and other small items placed at the front where you pay, this is deliberate. As you are on the queue, you are definitely going to look at most of those items, knowing your appetite and financial indiscipline, you are probably going to pick a few more items to buy. This is how you look at it from a customer point of view, *"Oh, they have this chocolate, I like it, since I have a few more bucks on the side, let get it"*. Most women will attest to that. Have you considered how the owners of the wholesale look at it? In his mind he is saying, *"Oh, this lovely customer of mine visited me today, and she is probably going to spend only ten bucks again today like she always do. How do I get her to spend twenty bucks this time? Oh yeah, she loves chocolates, let me put them next to the cashiers"*. The major reason behind putting these chocolates next to cashiers is not about convenience, it is about transaction frequency maximization. It is about how you make your customers buy more from you. It is about how you make your customers to keep buying from you. Be so good at what you do that your customers wants to keep coming back for more.

This is the only way you can grow your company from a ten customer company to a hundred Customer Company. This is how you can be able to move your company from a turnover of a few thousand bucks to a hundreds of thousands of bucks annually. It is possible. If you don't do it, someone else will do it and dominate the market and you won't like the results.

Cash flow Management

"It is simple, expenses have to go down and sales have to go up"

- Arun Iyer

It's really sad to hear about the statistics reporting on the numbers of businesses that close down on their first year. Some could suspect that a certain form of bad luck was somewhere in the corner facilitating the close down. Arguably so, it depends on what one believes. But all things being equal, if we can investigate the deaths of these businesses, we will shockingly find out the common serial killer behind their deaths. Just like oxygen is to the living organism, so is money to the business. The truth is, businesses close down for a very simple reason; they don't have any more money to keep their doors open.

This is not something that happens overnight, it is a process. Businesses don't suddenly die, they die over time. The moment the business begins to experience imbalanced movement of money in its systems, it begins to suffocate. We have said this at the beginning of the book that, *it is the small things that kills the gigantic businesses.* And, improper management of the company's cash flow is one of them. In fact, it is the greatest of them all. The health of your business is in its ability to use enough money to breath in order to make more money. Unlike the human being, for instance, the business doesn't have an automated cardiovascular system that ensures proper supply of oxygen around the body, it is banking on your decisions as the business manager to distribute money sufficiently around its systems for it to breath and make more money. Surprisingly, this is what most of us entrepreneurs struggles with most of the time; *progressive decision making*. We make haphazard decisions with money. We make a lot of *'money eating decisions'*. We are expenditure driven and not investment driven. Look, I believe most of us can attract certain amount of money at a given time, there is nobody in this day and age who can say that there is not even a single penny passing through their hands after a certain period of time.

The magic is not in starting a business, the magic is in staying in business. The greatest magic is when your business continue to exist and grow even better even long after you have died. This only happens when we have learnt to put money in the right places. It will only happen when we have managed to subdue ourselves to the knowledge and the understanding of putting money where it matters the most. Look, when you start a business, almost everything seem to matter to you. Just because something looks important means it matters. The first thing we need to understand with proper cash flow management more especially for start-up businesses as well as others is that we have to set our priorities right. What do we want to achieve and when do we want it achieved? The word cash flow is made out of two words, *cash* and *flow*. We have said it before somewhere in this chapter that we have to be investment driven. Investment means letting go of small amounts of money temporarily that you may have more in the future. Steven said *"begin with the end in mind"*. Financial wise, what kind of a company do you want to build? What needs to happen right now to get you enough resources to do other things that will get you closer to achieving your goal? Let your money flow in the direction of growth.

Let every penny that pass through your hand count. Let it be put where it will take the company further in the achievement of its goal. Don't overburden your budget. Keep your expenses small. Don't commit financially to things that you don't need at this present time. I have seen start-ups overburdened with expensive offices that they don't need. Some contracted big companies to lease expensive machines and equipment they didn't need at that level. Some hired a lot of people they don't need. Like I have said, there are so many things that will seem important to your eye when you start but they are not important to your company's growth and bottom line. The truth is that many start-ups are operating at a loss because all the monies they make monthly goes straight to servicing unnecessary financial commitments they have made. Because they are operating at a loss, they can't make enough money to be reinvested into the company's growth. The other truth is that, it is not all the months that you will make money. Some businesses makes money seasonally. And in the months where the company has no money coming in, its expenses will not be suspended. In the end, the company will have more money going out and no money coming in. Ultimately, the company has no more money to operate, and that's how great businesses with great business ideas dies if it's financial health is not taken good care of.

Invest in your financial literacy and asset management. It is very important. Buy books and other materials, attend seminars and training workshops that teaches about financial management and learn how to set financial goals for your company and how to achieve them. If you are careful, you will realize that all these things, leads generation, conversion, transactions frequency maximization and cash flow management are joined together to work hand in hand. You can't do them separately. It is a full strategy that should reflect all these things. When I look at your marketing strategy it should reflect on your projections. When you talk about cash flow management, I should see your leads generation and conversion strategies reflecting. You can do it

Mastery

When I was doing my last year at high school, one of my classmates invited me to join some little competition that they wanted me to participate in. When I agreed to enter the challenge they asked me this question, *"what is the longest word you know?"* For a few seconds I didn't know which word to think of, I thought of the name of this other guy I once read about in one of our Setswana books at primary school, his name was *Tsheganangwangwatsane.* We argued for a while because they wanted an English word. I decided to concede. I then asked them for the answer, one of the girls seating behind me shouted, *"supermasterblicationalism"*. I said *"what? That's not even English"*. They said, *"Yes, we made it up, in fact, our friends made it up"*. We argued for about half an hour about the word. Then I asked them for the meaning of the word. They said *"the ability to be so good at something that you do that everyone around you turns into experts by just watching you doing it"*. I nodded in agreement because somewhere in my subconscious mind I was flabbergasted. Look, the word may not exist in all the English dictionaries, but this made very good sense to me.

As an entrepreneur, whether a service provider or product developer, you need to reach a level of mastery in all the different areas of your business. You can't afford to do guess work all the time. You cannot afford to be mediocre at what you are doing. Sometimes we lose the market because we have built a very bad reputation in the market over the time through dissatisfying one customer after the other without even realizing it. When was the last time you walked into a restaurant and you didn't like the food or the culture, or the employees' attitude towards you and you walked out and never went back there ever again? Do you think they even noticed or remember that you did? Look, here is the thing, most businesses starts with one person, in most cases, that person is the one doing all the dirty work and all the administration work. If it is a graphics designing business, that same entrepreneur becomes the designer, the marketing manager, the accountant and everything else at the same time. Because the business is primarily based on what we call the *'craft of the business'* for its establishment, entrepreneurs tend to focus on gaining mastery on the side of the craft of the business than what we call the business of the craft. This is what we mean, when you are doing an energy drink business, the craft of your business will be the energy drink. The business of the craft, being the energy drink, means running an energy drink business.

A successful business is built through achieving mastery on both the craft of the business as well as the business of the craft. You need to master the skill of producing your product or service delivery. Above all, you need to be consistent in providing the market with the same if not an improved version of your value proposition. If clients came to you because they loved the experience they had with your service or product, or even through testimonials, they will want to come back for more to have a second round of the same experience. It will be greater if when they keep coming back they find an improved version of it. It will be disastrous for you if your customers tend to always have different inconsistent up and down experiences with your products or services. Today it was great, tomorrow bad. Imagine, ten customers comes to your business because they all heard the testimony of one person testifying on how great your services or your products are. And when they get to your business, they experience bad customer service and each one of them decides to testify against you to your other potential clients out there. We take this for granted a lot of times, but although word of mouth can grow a company's clientele base faster and cheaper, it can also destroy the company's clientele base if issues like this are not taken into proper consideration in the fastest possible time. Most big restaurants in the world are excelling in the restaurant business simply because they have managed to master their customer service by mastering the business of their crafts as well as the crafts of their businesses. They worked hard on identifying their unique value proposition which provided them with the niche they are now capitalizing on. But we should attribute their success in this industry solely on their ability to give each and every customer of theirs a special experience that made the customer to decide to make that business their new home for a while.

You don't just wake up and all of a sudden you have a properly oiled multifunctional machine ready to pump millions in revenues while creating a multigenerational impact that clients can't seem to consider going anywhere else anytime soon. You have to labor for it. Believe me, every other business out there can achieve this. If only we could understand that entrepreneurship is about creating profitable enterprises that can work without us having to be there, then we will realize that there is need for us to build system based business models than people based business models. Don't you ever feel that your business delivers better services or products to your level of satisfaction when you are the one doing the job hands on? Most of us have struggled with that for a very long time. I asked myself a question one day and I said, *"what will happen to my business if it happened that I died or somehow became incapable?"* Would this mean my business also dies? I missed many opportunities to travel or engage into so many projects because I didn't know how my business was going to survive without me being there. Okay let me be honest, I couldn't trust any of the guys I was working with at that time.

It was in that moment that I realized that I was not an entrepreneur yet, I was trapped in self-employment. I didn't have a business, the business had me. Why is it that even years after Steve Jobs had died, the Apple business is still running properly and even growing. Have you ever heard of anyone who complained that they didn't trust the chefs at KFC and preferred to have their meal prepared by Mr. Kentucky? Why is the KFC in your city tasting the same as the one in the other different cities and countries? Why is it that you have never inquired about who exactly cooked your meal at McDonald's? When you build your business based on you, your business will never grow beyond you. It will never deliver beyond your level of expertise. Even transactions frequencies will never exceed the capacity you can bear as an individual. This will consequently mean that the business will not (or should I say 'never') make a turnover bigger than the one it makes with the current annual transaction frequency. Even though we start the business alone doing almost everything, we need to seat down and map a way in which will see the business growing beyond us. Building the business systems will carry the business for years. Employees may come and go, but the business remains the same in the eyes clients and the rest of the target market.

We need to invest in laying out processes that will define clearly how our day to day business is going to be carried out. All processes must be clear and simple to be understood by anyone even without the need for further clarification by the next person. When you promise clients 10minutes turnaround time, you need to lay down a clear process that will realistically prove how what is going to go into what for what to happen until the client has your product in their hands in time you promised. It is easy to achieve high scores and ratings on delivery mastery when you are dealing with a smaller quantity of clients, but here is the thing, the more clients gets satisfied by your business the more they refer others to your business hence your clientele base growing. The growth may affect a lot of things that it may affect the normal operations of your business, but you need to gain mastery also on your communications skills and systems. All these systems works together to build a great relationship that you need to have with your customers. In the time that we exist in, all that clients wants it's a service or product that they can get cheaper, faster with better qualities. In setting yourself apart in the market, defining who you are in the market, you need to decide on which processes to employ to make your business work. When your business work, you don't have to work. The more you see yourself working very hard for things to move in your business, then your business is not working. As an entrepreneur, you need to see how your business is going to move you up the cash flow quadrant as defined by Robert Kiyosaki.

A lot of people will try to motivate you as you grow as an entrepreneur that there's a light at the end of the tunnel, but sometimes you don't know how long you have to walk in that tunnel until you see the light, in fact, the only light that you see is the one you left behind when you entered the tunnel and the more you walk the dimmer the light becomes behind you and the darker it gets before you.

CHAPTER 21

MANAGING CUSTOMERS & CLIENTS

"Get closer than ever to your customers. So close that you tell them what they need before they realize it themselves"

-Steve Jobs

Here is something you must understand, the shepherd does not multiply the flock, the flock multiplies the flock. If you don't take care of your customers & clients, someone else will. Success in entrepreneurship is measured by the size of your enterprise. With great and proper professional management of a small business, success is inevitable. We celebrate McDonald's today because they are the largest restaurant business worldwide. We hear success stories about them daily. Just in 2016 alone, over 600 franchises of McDonald's restaurants were opened in China alone. Look, this is not magic, it is a result of deliberate and conscious decision to build a system that works.

Ray Kroc, the man behind the success of this great McDonald's business, subscribed to certain principles which led to his success in this business. He bought the business from the McDonald's brothers and transformed it into this multi-billion dollar business that we see today. He transformed it via great strategic planning and thinking that had the customer/client at the center of it all. He built it from the time when it could only serve a few tens if not hundreds of people until it can now serve billions of people that it serves today in different countries and continents around the world.

Now, that's what we need to learn that we may know to apply it also in our businesses. I highly believe that in as much as this sound like rocket science to many, it doesn't mean that it is something we can't learn and master which will see our businesses transforming into globally competitive businesses in the future. It is good to admire great businesses that you admire, but I want you to know that you can also achieve what they achieved but in your area.

McDonald's was built to grow, from the start. It was not created for the owners, it was created for the customers. The most important people that directly keeps your business alive is your customers. Many businesses tend to forget that. In as much as getting into business has to be an act of augmenting the identified gap in the market, which can also be deemed as providing a solution to people's problems/challenges, you need to inculcate this belief within you that you need to continually improve your solution so that it adds value to a lot of people. Trust me, a satisfied customer is like wildfire, if one stick catches the flame, the whole bush will join in sooner than later. You don't need to be big to cause great fire, all you need is a little flame enough to make one stick burn. Just one customer can bring the whole community to your business.

Set your business for growth and success. Look, some people have gone to school for this, others learnt it through experience. A certain gentleman was interviewed and the interviewer asked him a question and said, *"what's the secret of your business success?"* the gentleman replied, *"great decision making"*. The interviewer then said, *"oh wow, nice, how did you become so good with making good decisions in business?"* , the gentleman slowly looked at her and said, *"by making many wrong decisions, now I know which decisions to make and which ones not to make"* . Experience is the best teacher. Let me add and say, not only your own experience can teach you, even other people's experiences should teach you something.

Other people have gone ahead of us in business so that they can learn the best way of doing things in business by making thousands and millions of mistakes so that we don't have to do them. Today they are very successful in their businesses, and we should learn from them also how they did it so that we can know to do it also. Their experiences taught them over a quite number of years, the same experience they have can teach us in much lesser time.

When you start a business you have two options;

1) To pursue profits now and loose the market later

2) To pursue the market now and again profits later

A certain gentleman once asked me to help him to host his seminar in my country, Botswana. He was from South Africa. So he wanted to bring his highly demanded services to Botswana. A lot of people were looking forward towards the seminar. They prayed day and night to get an opportunity to seat under his teaching. The people were ready. So it happened as I was helping him that only twenty seven people showed interest in the seminar. Twenty seven may sound like a very small number, but in my country, to get that number of people willing to pay the amount he was charging is unheard of.

He called me in the morning of the day of the event, everything was set, venue booked, accommodation for him booked, media invited, attendants ready, some of them travelled over ten hours to come to the main city for the event, some had to apply for leaves to avail themselves at the event, some had already sold some of their livestock to purchase the ticket. He called me and told me that he has decided not to come for the seminar. We had quite a lengthy discussion. The bone of contention was the fact that he mentioned that he decided not to come to Botswana for the event because he feels he was not going to make the profits he had intended on making. I expressed to him that Botswana is not like many countries out there. It is a growing country with a growing economy. Many people just recently awakened to the reality of so many opportunities out there for them in the world. Many things that are so common to majority of the people in the world are still new to them. The interest is there for them to pursue those opportunities, but there is so much skepticism surrounding many of the opportunities they are interested in.

If there was a person who was to benefit in the Botswana market for the longest time, was the person who is willing to invest so much time, energies and resources to prove himself to the market. I tried to show him that there are so many of his competitors who were eyeing the same opportunity that he was eyeing, and the only option that he could maximize was to prove himself first in the market, because when he has done that, Batswana are very loyal people. I remember saying this to him, *"You need to choose right now if you are willing to sacrifice the profits to gain the market later or sacrifice the market to gain the profits now.* But he chose the profits, he now lost the market to somebody else.

Even in marriage counseling sessions, they will tell you that *"it is better to lose an argument and win the person than to win the argument and loose the person".* We are in business to stay, and we don't just stay in business, we stay in business because of the continuous support we receive from our customers and clients. It is very important for us to learn the importance of working hand in hand with our customers and clients to build our businesses. You need to see a way of continually improving yourself to serve your customers better. I love what Richard Brandson once said, which is the philosophy surrounding his business success, *"take care of your employees, they will take care of your customers"*.

You need to find a way, a philosophy that ensures that your customers and clients receives the best hospitality in your business. You need to find processes that ensures that your customers are happy with your service delivery. You need to find a culture that you are willing to invest towards establishing in your business to ensure that your customers feels welcome and dignified in your business. Treat your business like a new relationship. Ensure maximum customer satisfaction always. Rather lose the profit for that time and gain a client than to insist on making a profit at that time and loose the client. Clients talks. Their talks travels faster. Do everything in your power to reduce bad publicity. There is a saying that says *"people may forget what you did for them but they will never forget how you made them feel"*.

CHAPTER 22

BUILD AN EFFECTIVE & PROPER TEAM

"You don't build a business, you build people, then people will build the business"

-Unknown

The quality of the success of any entrepreneur is determined by the quality of his/her team. One of the powerful quotes I have ever met in my life says *"if you want to walk fast, walk alone. But if you want to go far, go with others"*. Most of entrepreneurs are good with coming up with awesome ideas but fail dismally in the business because of their support structures. The most immediate support structure for most entrepreneurs is their team. The team is your extension as the entrepreneur. Building a team is not just a simple casual work of putting people together. It requires more than just recruiting people to work with you. I have personally learnt this skill the hard way.

The habit of *Beginning with the End in Mind* was introduced more than 25 years ago by Dr. Stephen R. Covey in his groundbreaking bestseller, The 7 Habits of Highly Effective People. Many entrepreneurs have applied this great skill across different areas of their entrepreneurial ambitions and achieved tremendous results in their entrepreneurial journey. I still believe that this skill will work for many of us when it comes to building teams for our businesses. Begin with the end in mind. You need to ask yourself, what is it that you want to achieve at the end of the day? You need to lay out that picture down. If you need to use virtual aids please use them, whichever way, you have to have a clear picture of exactly what you want to achieve. After you clear out the picture of your goal, then you have to ask yourself this question; *'what has to happen for this picture to become a reality?'*

What processes needs to be employed for the goal to be achieved in the time that it has been set for it? Asking yourself this questions will open your eyes to see a lot of things about your company's goals. After you clear out the processes that needs to be employed then you need to ask yourself about the skills that are needed for such processes to be employed. That's when you can now ask yourself about who has those skills that you need for your company and they carry the kind of character that can easily make working with them and other team mates more efficient. Everybody has to look forward to come to work. You build the environment of your business by first building the team through the recruiting characters that you need.

For me character comes before skill. They say *"skills may take you up the ladder, but only character can keep you there"*. You don't recruit someone because they want to join your team, you recruit them because they have something in them that will add value to what your company is set to achieve. Recruit people that you can take into what you want them to be. It is your vision, although you need to welcome different opinions and ideas from your team to build a magnificent company, you still need to have a footing on the direction of the company. Avoid hiring family members within the executive management of your company, unless they are willing to work fully invested in your vision. It's easy to work with them, but it's hard to fire them or admonish them when matters necessitates that you do because they have their own way of taking everything personal. Some people call it *entitlement mentality syndrome*. Avoid hiring people who are not better than you at what you are hiring them to do, unless if they have the potential to grow to be far much better than you.

When you start a business alone, the most immediate person to be in the company is the CEO. Oh yes, you have been looking forward to it. In fact, some people started businesses because they wanted to their own CEO(s). There's nothing wrong with that. Here is the thing, before you get too much about being your company's CEO, you are actually right, you should be the CEO, the Chief Everything Officer. Hold on a second about the Chief Executive Officer because I'm not sure if you are one just yet.

I've said this somewhere in this book that, you need to walk the walk you are going to hire someone else to walk in your company before they do. This is beyond the fact that when you start you can't afford to have staff members but the fact that you need to get first-hand experience of how that job is done. You cannot manage someone better at something when you don't know how that job is done and how it feels like doing that job. You need to achieve your own mastery alone. You have to do the dirty work yourself first, the administration and every other thing. You work on the first customer alone. You perfect the processes. You weed out what needs to be weeded out.

Remember, starting with the end in mind, you get to realize the things that needs to be done in your company while you are doing it alone first. As your monthly revenue increases, you let go of another task and hire someone else with the right skill and experience to take care of that task. The more you do this, you gain momentum. Your capacity grows. Hire the most important people first. Do you know the most important skill in business? Come 'on. Yes, selling. Hiring is about increasing your capacity to manage your demand and supply easily. And to up the demand, somebody has to generate the business in the market. This is why you have to hire sales people first. Then once your demand increases, you can let go of another task and hire someone else to take care of it. This is not done haphazardly, it is done following the habit of beginning with the end in mind.

Then you can graduate to *Chief Energy Officer* to manage the energies of your team to ensure that everyone else is doing what they are supposed to do in the manner which is expected. This is the level we need to strive to reach. It is the level just before the one where you can now have a business that can work without you. If you hire a new CEO, then chances are that you are not needed in that business anymore for it to work. Do you know what does that mean for you? Scaling. Yes, replanting the same model you have developed in other location just the same way it is and hiring a new set of a team, same structure but different faces. You know why? The model is already tested and proven.

Of course, you may need to change here and there to suit the location, but the major part of the job you have already done it while you were the Chief Everything Officer. Now you can call yourself the Executive Chairman, like Jack Ma. You can engage investors to help you scale up your businesses, then have them in your board. Or you can chose to move into a completely new business and start from scratch. But here is the thing, businesses may be different but the principles of business success remains the same. If they be observed on the left hand side, what happened on the right hand side will happen on the left hand side.

Your business success will be determined by your ability to follow this simple but complex science of business growth.

CHAPTER 23

YOU ARE NOT ABOUT ONE THING

When was the last time somebody reminded you to focus on one thing? Focus is what they will keep advising you to do when you are pursuing your dreams. I was writing this portion of the book seating at a top table with very powerful young people, amongst them, my all-time inspiration, Kagiso Morebodi, the young inspirational man who inspired me to follow my dreams. I remember I used to wake up every single morning and go through his Facebook timeline to check whether he has updated any uplifting post like he always did. I was always looking up to his next post. Let me get to the point. Almost every successful entrepreneur will attribute their success to their ability to focus. But here is the thing, it is not focus that we have a problem with, it is our understanding of the word *"focus"* that gives us the problem with our ability to focus.

We exist in a generation with entrepreneurs who are armed with more than one idea that can shape the world. We can talk of the likes of *Elon Musk, Sir Richard Brandson* and others. Serial entrepreneurs. I can boldly talk about this because I used to suffer from the same problem. If there is a fight I have always had with my brother, *Moagisi Zulu Gokatweng* (founder of Native Foods) for many years, it is the issue of focus. Today I will tell him that I want to do this, with all the greatest excitement in the world, the following week I will be coming back to him with other idea. For many years, I had accumulated so many great ideas but in the end I have none implemented. I've had great ideas since I was fourteen which big corporations are making millions of bucks with today on monthly basis.

It is in my nature, my head flows with dozens of ideas on weekly basis. I can't help it. I could have long been a Millionaire. But unfortunately being a millionaire is not only about having a great million dollar business idea, it is about your ability to have a great idea that you are willing to commit yourself to implement and grow it to success. But here is the thing, we are different. There are people who have only one business idea or can be defined by just one business idea, like *Mark Zuckerberg* for *Facebook*, which is not entirely true because Mark had many ideas before Facebook. In fact, even within Facebook, I believe Mark always gets new ideas on how to improve Facebook on daily basis.

There are people who gets business ideas across different industries. Great ideas that can add value to the lives of people and generate millions in revenue. Ideas with commercial value. For example, today you get an idea to package frozen cooked meals for the busy bachelors in the city, you get so excited about it and you see yourself as a millionaire. Tomorrow you get an idea to buy bicycles and attach buckets to them and run around the city with a few more guys doing a mobile car wash. The same millionaire feeling comes to you. The next day you think of opening a guesthouse in the northern parts of Botswana to benefit from the traffic of tourists traveling to Botswana to see the biggest inland delta in the world. It's your nature, your mind is always in the move. Your eyes sees opportunities everywhere.

Let me tell you the truth, you are not wrong. Yes, you are not normal. You are very special. There is not many of you like that. And it's okay to be like that. The only thing that's missing on you is the intelligence or the ability to be able to pursue your dream and see them becoming a reality and growing them into one of the world's greatest successes. Look, you will not be the first, there are people who have managed to do that. There is that power in you to do that. I'm not saying you can do everything you think of. Because truth be told, some ideas you get, it's like some relationships that you were denied the chance to be involved in, you will realize as time goes on that they were not worth it. But in the midst of all these legion of ideas, there are some, more than one that you can concurrently pursue to success because people of our generation can.

Focus could mean a lot of things. It depends on who you are. To people with one idea, their struggle with focus is often premised on their ability to gather the energies to pursue the goal to the end. To those with more than one idea, the creative, the innovative, their struggle is primarily premised on their ability to silence their minds from other ideas so that they may be able pursue the one they currently have or to formulate a strategy that will enable them to pursue more than one idea at once.

Many books that I know of have addressed the issue of focus, but I believe they left out this group of serial entrepreneurs. They didn't fully scratch the itch to the satisfaction of those that I have interacted with.

Before we go any further, it is very important that we understand that business has different growth stages. There is the starting phase, there is the growth phase, and there is the sustenance phase. All these stages requires different forms of focus. Almost every day of your entrepreneurship journey you are going to fight the war of focus. But here is the question, what exactly do you focus on? I believe that, from my vantage point, the greatest ability that has taken a lot of people far in business is their ability to prioritize well. You need to learn how to set your priorities well. If you are at the starting stage, you may be having a great idea you want to do, the truth is that you are going to get a lot other ones that seem equally important and profitable like the one you already have.

Just like in relationships, there is always going to be someone who is better looking than your woman/man. You need to embrace this fact. If your goal is to marry the most beautiful girl in the world, chances are that you will never marry because every single day you will always find someone more beautiful that the one you thought she is more beautiful. The most beautiful girl will be the one that you have to fully convince yourself that she is the one, and you are willing to embrace the fact that you are going to stick with her for the rest of your life. Of course there is so many other factors that needed to be put in perspective to aid your choice. Similarly, you need to do the same if you are struggling with this multiple business ideas paralysis. Look into your purpose, find the business idea that resonates with who you are. I can tell you, amongst those many ideas there is one or some that are in alignment with what you feel is the original intent of God that backed up your birthing into this world.

The other factor that you need to keep in mind is that you need to look into ideas that can be grown to accommodate the creation of other supporting businesses that are also in alignment with your purpose. The idea is to start with an idea that can produce profits that can be reinvested into another business idea which will also produce other profits which can be reinvested into yet another idea in your pipeline. You are not supposed to do this haphazardly, but you need to do it with proper plan. The reason why a lot of people feel that this can't work is because some tried it but tried it the wrong way and now no one trusts it because a lot of people have failed it many times before.

To do this with ease, I suggest you list all your ideas and form a strategy on how you are going to implement them one by one. Eliminate those that which sounds really good but they are not realistic. Put to one group those that resonates with your passion, goals, skills, gifts and purpose. The one that you feel you can do naturally. Steve Jobs says *"we cannot connect the dots going forward, we can only do so looking backwards"*. I want to attempt to derive some logic I never saw in this statement for a while, I don't know how you are going to take it but this is what I got, Jesus made a very powerful statement in the Bible and said *"you do not understand what I am doing right now, but one day you will understand"*. I believe that there is so much beauty in the unveiling of great things out of prolonged obscurity and curiosity.

As an entrepreneur, you first need to know the full picture of your exact goal. At the end of it all, what exactly do you want to have built? You need to be able to dissect your goal into small parts and see how your ideas that you have can feed into each other to grow into the picture. It is Will Smith who said *"if you want to build the strongest wall, don't set out to build the strongest wall, set out to lay each brick so perfectly until the last brick and you will have the strongest wall"*. As aforementioned in the other chapters, excellence is the ultimate result of the attention paid to each detail of the whole component. Don't look at your wall as a wall, look at it as well arranged bricks. You can't lay more than one brick with both of your hands at the same time. Learn to give attention to what needs to be done perfectly at the current time. Keep your mind of the wall and your eyes in the brick. That's what I call focus.

You may start with one thing but that's not your end. You need to continually seek for ways to improve your portfolio, products, services and your general value proposition to the market. There is so many things you can always do to augment what you already have. Studies have proved that inform doubles almost every year. The market evolved every single month. Technology is shaping the world in the faster way that is still fascinating a lot of us. Big corporations sleeps today and wake up insignificant because technology has given the small freshmen the platform to build better value proposition to the market. When your business objective is clear, your choices will always align themselves to the company's purpose. It will be easy to decide on which idea to incorporate into your vision. In business you are not only faced with the challenge to improve yourself, you are also faced with competitors who are willing to continually improve themselves to serve the market better. Your failure to take a lead or at least keep up with this may sabotage the future of your business. But my desire is that you may reach a level of strategically achieving all your goals without confusion and wastage.

Improve yourself, you are not about one thing. There's always one more thing you can enterprise. But the key thing is to learn the art of finishing everything you have started. It doesn't matter how many things you have started, our multitasking abilities are not the same, but what matters is that you have to finish all that you start. Be spontaneous. Have new features in your business. Don't be boring. Find interesting things that will continually improve your solution that you may continue to be relevant in the market for the longest time. Imagine the time you joined Facebook, does it look the same way today? Definitely not. For those of you who want to run groups of companies, serial entrepreneurship is so fun. Keep looking on the next project to embark on.

But here is the key, no matter how many babies you want to have, you can never have them all at once. You give birth to one today, you raise him for a while until he can do a certain things and stable in his growth then you can make another one. Until and until. Richard Brandson has done this and he is still doing it. Bishop Tudor Bismarck is doing this opening churches around the world. The world is your village. You need to expand to the other parts of the world. You are not about one office. You are not about one employee. You are not about one car? You are not about one product. No Sir. You are bigger than you think. You are not about the small market even though you start with it.

Think big and start small. Though your beginning may be small, your ending is bigger and better. My mentor BF Rams says *"today's champions were yesterday's amateurs"*. Facebook used to only have a few members from a certain university at some point as their total membership, but today almost over a billion people are on Facebook around the world. Coca-Cola sold only 25 bottles in their first year, but today over a billion cans of Coca-Cola are being consumed daily around the world. Jeff Bezos used to run around selling books on Amazon, but he knew within himself that he is not about one thing, he wanted to make Amazon *"The everything store"* and today Amazon sells almost everything online. You may start with one thing today, but you are not about one thing. You can do more. You can venture into other industries you never imagined. You can venture into many new ways of deploying your products and services to your target market.

I heard about the story of a certain Indian young man a few months ago. True story. He opened a business to sell coconuts in his village. His business was really suffer because many other vendors selling coconuts had taken a larger market share. One day a group of Americans came and connected the internet in his village. The young man spent his time learning about a lot of things at the computer labs when the rest of the people went to the market to sell. He learnt different thing ranging from how to operate a computer to surfing the internet. He learnt until he managed to open an online store that sells coconuts. He started receiving orders from countries as far as America. He became the largest international coconut distributor that he had to buy coconuts that used to sell more than him to sell them internationally online.

You are not about one thing. When the goal seems not to be amounting to anything, don't change the goal, change the strategy. You are not about one strategy. Keep finding ways to do your business better and serve bigger quantities of clients better.

CHAPTER 24

SORT YOUR BREAD & BUTTER

"Do what you have to do until you can do what you want to do"

-Oprah Winfrey

The truth of the matter is that entrepreneurship is hard, it is difficult. You are a living organism, you need to eat. Your dream will take time to reach fruition. Your dream will take time to feed you. One of the challenges that affects a lot of entrepreneurs around the world in their quest to achieve their entrepreneurial ambitions is the issue of the bread and butter. As an entrepreneur, you need to ask yourself this question; what value can you exchange in the meantime so that you can survive to keep existing so that you can do what you want to do?

Do something that will put food in your stomach, shelter over your head, clothes in your back. It doesn't have to be in line with the dream that you are trying to achieve, it just have to have the capacity to give you a few dollars at the same time allowing you the time to follow your dreams. You need to take care of yourself. Get into the cash cow businesses. Sell something. You have to be smart with it. There are so many quick-cash businesses that you can try out so that they can give you enough money enough to live on while you are still building your long term vision. You have to find something that can give you a few dollars in the meantime while you are still trying to break even. Look into your talents, skills and abilities. How many of them are you willing to utilize so that they can earn you a few bucks to live on every month? You can also consider trading those skills with other established entrepreneurs so that you can add value to their companies while they compensate you enough to pursue your dreams.

Do whatever it takes to make money on the side to feed yourself. This will allow you the opportunity to be able to reinvest the profits into your company's growth and not your sustenance. Don't be counted amongst the statistics of entrepreneurs who are blocking their company's growth because of their need live hand to mouth? You make a hundred bucks today, and you have to choose between increasing your production and feeding your hungry stomach. Separate the business's money from your personal money. Use your company's money to grow the company and use the money you make on the side to finance your bread and butter. It's hard, but you have to do it.

CHAPTER 25

DON'T QUIT NOW, QUIT THE DAY AFTER TOMORROW

Jack Ma, the founder of Alibaba, one of the greatest entrepreneurs of our time said something powerful, he said, *"today is bad, tomorrow is worse, but the day after tomorrow is beautiful. But a lot of people quit tomorrow evening"*. You might have heard this a countless times before, a lot of people have a tendency of quitting few miles away from reaching their destinations. Few phone calls away from the deal. Few meetings away from the deal. Few interviews away from the appointment. Few handshakes away from the right hand shake. Few seminars away from 'the' seminar. Few more doors away from the deal.

Of course, it is understandable. You have been trying for the longest time now. Some people have embarked into the same journey you are in and they have overtook you and they seem like they have all their ducks in a row. You are tired. There is not even one tiny bit of energy left in you to press on. But guess what, as Dr. Magang has said before in the previous chapters, only those who endure to the end shall enjoy the fruits of their perseverance. Don't quit now, quit the day after tomorrow, for if you reach to that day you will realize that you almost made a permanent decision in a temporary situation.

CHAPTER 26

STAY ALIVE

"Most people are not destroyed by the external storms going on in their lives, they are destroyed by the conversations going on in their mind about their lives"

- Boago F. Rams

Sometimes when we talk about entrepreneurship, we get caught up in talking about different terms and concepts diagnosing and tackling problems that are to deal with the enterprise itself and not the entrepreneur. In as much as there are reports and statistics reflecting the numbers of companies that dies every year, there are countless cases where many entrepreneurs are reported dead. Well, I'm fully aware that people die and entrepreneurs are not exempted. But I'm highly persuaded to believe that some of these deaths can be avoided. It pains me to learn that majority of these deaths are cases of suicide. Many people will never understand, the pressure and the pain that comes with the whole package of entrepreneurship. Many people know entrepreneurship as a glorious thing that people enjoy enough to be putting on nice suits every day, sleeping in huge beautiful houses and driving big cars. There are people that still kill themselves still having those things.

Entrepreneurship is hard. That's what makes it fun to others while depressing to others. I wish I could say it is easy. In this journey you will make very bad decisions on the way, no matter how vigilant and careful you may be. Many of your expectations will not come out as you expected them to be. Some things will never make sense. Some things will turn against you. But in all these things, you need to know and never forget that you are more than a conqueror. You need to invest in your emotional intelligence. You need to know the difference between you and your company. When your company has problems, although you feel like you and your company are indivisibly intertwined, you need to know that it has problems and not you. When your company owes, it owes, not you. Never be afraid to fail, no matter how big.

I know of a certain gentleman, he was running a business. He believed so much in the business that he got pre-orders from people. The business failed and he couldn't pay the people's money back. He got an idea to do another one, he risked it all on this second one because he believed in it, he got pre-orders again and went big, everything calculated to the point, the plan was to make more money to pay back other debts made years ago, the business failed again. An old man who got into so many debts trying to achieve his goal of owning an international standard business, he started this business when he was on his 30s after serving as an employee for a long time, he failed in this business so many times that he got depressed, on his late 50s, he tried the business again that was going to make him a great success if it succeeded or triple his problems if it failed, the business failed, he killed himself.

There are so many great entrepreneurs around the world taking their precious lives every single year. Some cases may not be reported, but the world is losing so many great and talented people every year due to suicide. I want to speak to you who are still alive today, you need to take care of yourself. Suicide is not only when you blow off your brains with a gun or when you hang yourself, you may die of depression or heart attack, and you may die because of poor diet. You need to invest in your health. You need to invest in your mental health. You may not see it, but you are the most important part of your business. You have a lot to offer this world. The world hasn't seen your best yet. When you are in trouble, no matter how bad it is, killing yourself should not be an option.

Do whatever you can to stay alive. Surround yourself with the people who makes you happy. Don't do business alone, partner with people who can share with you the pressures of the business when they come. Have think tanks. Be part of mastermind groups. Have a mentor. Someone who is experienced in what you are doing. Take time out, breath. It's okay to relax. I used to struggle with resting. I felt like I'm wasting so much time. I felt like I'm wasting myself and my life. In fact, whenever I thought I was resting, I was not resting at all. I would be doing something else. I would rest from my company's duties and do my NGO duties. Or I will not go to the office and spend the entire day working from home. I thought I was losing when I rested, until I learnt that I wasn't loosing, I was gaining.

Take care of yourself. Take care of your mind. Take care of your emotions. Take care of your peace. It is your responsibility to do it. You have a lot to offer the world. Some of the things you are going to try will not work. Some of them will take you into some serious deep trouble. But when they do, always remember that you are just an innocent kid from your mother's house who believed enough that there could be a better life out there and pursued it. This is why you have to have a relationship with a supreme being. A relationship with God.

If there's something that will keep you closer to God in life is entrepreneurship. Say your prayers in the simplest of the words you can find and tell God what you want. Ask him to help you. Ask him to help you stay alive. I have noticed, every time I pray, I may not get the answer I want, but I get the peace of mind I need, and in the peace of my mind I usually get so many ideas on how to calm the storms of my life. I believe life is just a test of the amount of pressure you can take, the more pressure you take, the more impact you make. The world is banking on you to take enough pressure to rescue them from their challenges. Don't let yourself die with the solution to their problems, believe and keep pursuing. Stay alive, stay pushing and stay winning.

CHAPTER 27

ACT LIKE A PROSTITUTE

CHAPTER 27

ACT LIKE A PROSTITUTE

"These days, the business is not in what you sell, but in how you sell it"

-Goitsemang J. Khutsafalo

I think we owe it to ourselves as entrepreneurs around the world to have this conversation. When Sir Richard Branson registered his company as a 16 years old boy, the regulators wrote back to him and told him that he can't call his business 'Virgin' because the word sounded rude. He said this when he was in Botswana in a meeting which I had the opportunity to be part of where he was sharing his story with the audience. He said he really wanted this name and went on to research more about it. He said he wrote back to the regulators and told them that they were wrong. The word 'Virgin' actually means 'pure, untouched, unblemished, whole' and many other things. They registered the Virgin Group. And we know the amazing disruptive businesses that were built by Sir Richard Branson after that moment to date.

I think that if we need to see a perfect picture that will resemble 'thinking like an entrepreneur and acting like a prostitute', Sir Richard Branson will be that perfect example. Despite all the odds that were against him as a little boy and as he was growing as a young entrepreneur who barely had nothing like most us, he still pressed on to build what we see today as a multinational multi-billion dollar British company that is worth over 19.5 billion US Dollars and controls over 400 companies today. Since we talked about disruption, I personally believe that disruption happens when a product or a service can save the customer time, energy and resources. More especially when the customer can get a good quality product/service cheaper, faster and better. During the conversations with Sir Richard Branson, he said it himself, *"go after the things that you feel you can do better than those who are currently doing it, no matter how big and misbehaving they are"*. If you do that, what leads millions of men to brothels around the world, can lead a legion of them to your own too.

We live in the times far much different from any other time in the past. The world has never been wealthier that it is today. As we speak, the Gross World Product has averaged US$107.5 trillion in 2014 as compared to the US$33.54 trillion recorded in 2000. We can see with our eyes that technology fueled by the internet hasn't only changed how we live our day to day life, it has also changed how we do business in today's world. We can never beat technology. We don't have to. The internet as Vusi Thembekwayo would say is *'a catalyst for change'*. We can only position ourselves to benefit from the growth it brings to the business world every day. I asked a question before in a workshop I was speaking at in Limpopo (South Africa), I said, *"did you know that in your simple 5 minutes trip from your house to this venue, there were approximately 100 companies involved in facilitating that 'simple' trip?"* They all looked at me for a few seconds with baffled faces. I could see that they were counting the ones they could remember.

Suddenly, the smiles began to show again in their faces when the list went on. Most of us when we look at the business world, we look at it from the consumer point of view that all that our eyes can see is what we can consume, we don't look at the business world from the value addition (entrepreneurship) point of view to see what people need that we can provide. I will ask you this, when last did you met a need in someone's life? Write this down; *you will not succeed in business because you created a great product/service, you will only succeed because you sold it the right way it is supposed to be sold.* Success is not in the craft of the business only, it is premised in the business of the craft. There are so many entrepreneurs out there, but here is the thing; an entrepreneur with a 'small idea' and a great business mindset will defeat an entrepreneur with a great idea and a small business mindset any day.

Studies says of all the things that you can do, 45% of what you do, everybody else out there can do it the same way you are doing it, the other 45% of what you are able to do, others can do it far much better than you can do, and the last remaining 20% is the things that only you can do like no one else can. I know that when we think of a prostitute, most of us picture some lady under a street light in a dark corner somewhere. Or in front of a hotel along the road. The Nigerians will tell you, in Lagos, although prostitution is illegal in Nigeria, you will find prostitutes almost everywhere in some avenue at night.

I don't know about you, but when I picture the business world in a few years to come, I see nothing but stiff competition that's going to swallow many entrepreneurs alive. We read about *'the survival of the fittest' at* our junior school, and I can assure you, we may not be different tribes fighting with bows and arrows today, but I can tell you this, the battle that we are in with our entrepreneurial endeavors is not a joke. There are so many cutting edge products and services that are coming in the future that if you don't transposition yourself today you might experience what other tech-victims experienced in the past. They say *"if you can't be the man, you will work for the man"*.

The war has taken a different toll. You may be thinking of trade wars at governmental levels, but hear this, although that may be the case with other countries, entrepreneurship at any level has always been about a fight for territorial dominion. One thing I know for sure about a woman is that you can mess with anything that she has, but don't dare come near her territory. She will defend it with anything, even her own life included. Dominion. In the prostitution industry, there are 2 types of prostitutes. There are those who are victims, and there are those who are 'entrepreneurs' (for lack of a better word). Statistics shows that about 25% of prostitutes around the world are those who were trafficked into prostitution by pimps. I hear that most 'sex workers' (as they will be often referred to) that works for pimps can be paid around $5 - $10 per 'gig'.

In my research, I have learnt about another lady in Los Angeles (names withheld). She makes around $500 - $1'000 a night in a tough day. On a good day, she can go up to $8'000 a night. And here is the thing, pimps hates women like her who work for themselves because they want to get all that money to themselves and pay them peanuts. Every prostitute has a corner. Territory. Many sex workers who work for themselves get beaten up, harassed and even killed in their corners.

This lady suffered all that, but guess what? She won't quit. No matter what happened last night, the next day she will show up, dressed up and ready to 'conquer the world again'. And guess what? She doesn't just show up, she shows up differently all the time. She shows up stronger and wiser. There's a reason why customers keeps coming to her every night. Imagine how far we could be as entrepreneurs if this was the same mentality that we had towards our businesses and our market share in the industry.

I believe this is the part of the book you have been longing to get to. I just hope that in the midst of your curiosity, you didn't just jump to this chapter without considering the other chapters before this one. But I will understand if you did. I remember the faces of people every time I mentioned the name of this book. I believe we have just registered a new *Frequently Asked Question* worldwide; '*Act like a what?*'. Trust me, I totally understand. I felt exactly like that when I first got the idea of this book. You will never understand the value of where someone is going until you understand where they are coming from. For years, I have personally struggled in business. Sometimes we sing about how a great blessing it is to be born in Africa, but the sad truth is that sometimes we get that feeling every now and then that maybe, just maybe, being born here was a huge curse.

We find ourselves existing in a world we don't even understand how it works and expect ourselves to win even though we play against systems that have been there for years. In fact, the very same systems that pioneered the trends that we see around us. Some of us that are passionate about entrepreneurship, we keep trying things every now and then but we always come down to asking ourselves the same question, *"what am I doing wrong?"* and even up to now we still haven't found the answers. We are trying to solve the problems and we can't solve any because the problem we think is the problem isn't really the problem, we are. *Think like an Entrepreneur, Act like a Prostitute* felt like the answer to me. Since so far you know how entrepreneurs thinks like, let's deal with what you bought this book for.

Prostitution. Let's face it, this is a conversation worth having. Not for its controversy, but for the wisdom hidden behind it that entrepreneurs around the world can learn from.

Like I have said in the beginning of this book, there is so much to learn and so much to do with what we learn from this book. Since we are talking about 'acting', let me take this opportunity to say this here. The magic is not in knowing, the magic is in putting action to what we know. Action is what differentiates successful people from the rest. You will be surprised if you were to discover that the same person you admire became your inspiration simply by continually applying the same knowledge that you carry in your head which you are doing nothing about.

There is a quote I heard from one of my mentors that says *"successful people do every day what unsuccessful people do occasionally"*. Entrepreneurship is about results. It is about the outcomes. What really inspires us about other entrepreneurs around the world isn't really the big things they have achieved, but the wisdom they applied to transform the small things they had into the big things that we see today, most of time building these successes in the midst of all kinds of hopeless situations and tribulations.

Business in today's world isn't really about what you are selling, it is about how you are selling it that matters the most. For some of you who are running businesses, let me ask you this; what is your competitor doing that is keeping him ahead of you in your industry? Or let me put it this way, if you were your own competitor, how were you going to kick yourself in the butt? I don't expect you to answer the questions right now, but if you can, please take time and attend to these questions.

The world has completely transformed. Technology hasn't just changed how we interact with the world today in our daily lives, it has also changed how we do business today. It has changed our priorities. It has turned our preferences around. What used to matter in the days past doesn't even matter at all today. And most of these same things that don't matter today were investments of other people in the form of businesses, and technology just rendered them irrelevant in one night. All these trends are because there are thousands and millions of entrepreneurs around the world seeking to continually re-invent their solutions or invent new solutions to keep up with the ever changing needs of the people around different markets of the world. There is so much fierce competition from all corners, and I'm telling you, there is no how you can survive it if you can't act like a prostitute.

As we had already discussed in the opening of this book, David Joseph Schwartz once said that *"How we think shows through in how we act. Attitudes are mirrors of the mind. They reflect thinking"*. Of course, in a very real sense, given what we know about prostitutes, we may find it difficult to make sense of this topic. But if you allow me a few more minutes, I will try the best that I can to hit home run with this topic.

Let's face it. Prostitutes don't make money by having great sex with you. They make money by having sex with as many people as they can in the shortest time possible. Here is the logic, perhaps what may sound like the 'secret'; ***the same product or service versus multiple recipients with focus on the transactions and production of recurring business***. That is what is happening here. Stay with me. The idea is not to get into business but to stay in business. It is staying in business which balances and grows the cash flow. The cash flow's life cycle is determined by the transaction frequencies. And here is the thing, it our job now to learn how to manage the cash flow by keeping our margins high and our expenses low, in practical ways through the activities that we do everyday in our businesses. Keep in mind that the enjoyment of the service is not prioritized on the prostitute but the customer even though on certain occasions the satisfaction is mutual.

There is just so much we can talk about, but right now we will focus on the transaction frequencies. Did you know, companies are deemed to be small or big based on the size of two things;

Customer base

Workforce

Revenues are consequential. Let us look at it this way. You are considered a small business because you are serving a small number of customers. And because you serve a small number of customers, which could be justified by the size of your capacity, which is determined by the size of your workforce, you can then make a considerable small number of transactions because of the small number of customers, which translates into small amounts of revenue. It is this simple but complicated cycle which has kept small businesses small. We have a lot of entrepreneurs working hard every single day today just to meet their monthly working capital. There are no structures and strategies in place to ensure that the company experiences growth at specific given times. Most entrepreneurs live hand to mouth.

Most entrepreneurs have businesses where they (as the owners of the businesses) are the major constituent of the company's business processes, without them, the business can't even operate. It is sad, although many reasons can be given to justify this situation, but the fact remains that companies built on this kind of foundations can never grow beyond the entrepreneur. Do you remember the 3 P(s) of business that we discussed earlier? People, process and product? Every business has to be scalable. It has to grow. It has to work without you. It has to be able to operate in a such a way in which customers comes to your business and they get assisted by somebody else and they get the same customer satisfaction that they would have gotten if they were to be assisted by you. Every start-up has to be built to grow. It has to be set-up to grow, from the beginning.

Hear me, I know how difficult it is to scale-up, more especially when it has to deal with having to entrust someone else with the running of the business. Control. We hate 'losing control'. If we look closely, we don't have a problem with scaling, our biggest problem is having to deal with control issues. Why would we rather do it ourselves all alone? Because we have different types of fears. *"What if I teach them and then they run off stealing my business?" "I can't trust no one with my business, I just can't"*. I will not dwell much on this, but I want you to see that whatever reason that we may give ourselves here leaves us with one thing, you having to be the sole engine and every other part of your business that keeps it alive. Limiting your capacity, limiting your transactions, limiting your revenues. Let's look at this statement one more time; *the same product/service versus multiple recipients with focus on the transactions and production of recurring business.* Do you realize that business is about repeating the same thing so perfectly to multiple people and doing it so well every time you repeat it so that you can be given another chance to repeat it again and you get paid each time you repeat it? That's all it is.

If we zoom closely into the same sentence, we will see another reflection that will give us more insight in becoming profitable business people, entrepreneurs that think like one and acts like a prostitute. When you look at the statement, we see the reflection of *'the craft of the business'* and *'the business of the craft'*. Every business is about mastering these two. Unfortunately, most of us as entrepreneurs we only perfect our skills only on the side of the craft of the business. The craft of the business is that product or service that you will produce to meet the need you have identified in the market. Most of the time we only focus on being so good with either producing this product or rendering this service. We neglect the other important part of managing a profitable business. Look, a great product alone won't build a successful profitable start-up.

I have seen so many start-ups with great products and services having to close their doors, not because the product was bad, no, because the entrepreneur running the business focused only on mastering the craft of his business and neglected the business of his craft. Have you ever wondered? Why is it that when you get into business as a programmer or a designer at first, and you are the one programming or designing in the business, if this business grows, you the programmer or designer that started it you will automatically be forced to graduate to a level of managing this enterprise that programs or design? Called CEO? This is to show you, the most important job for you as the entrepreneur to do is to master the two phases of your entrepreneurial journey; the phase where you should be concerned about doing both the craft of the business and the business of the craft for your business and the phase where now you will be more focused only on the business of your craft. Take *Mark Zuckerberg* for example. He is the guy that coded and crafted Facebook, the moment it grew to this point, what do you think he is concerned with? Yes, the business of his craft. Commercializing. Generating value or revenue out of what he has created. Managing the vision for the company and ensuring that the company does not deviate from it. He has people who are coding and taking care of the craft of his business.

Each and every customer or client that you will ever have deserves the same great experience that you will ever give to any other customer or client. Each and every customer or client you will ever have deserves the best from your company. This can be achieved by a simple tip, if you could manage to repeat the same process that gave one client a great customer satisfaction to every other client that you will ever have. *"The same product or service versus multiple clients..."* But the problem with most start-ups today is that we fail to repeat the same great thing that we did last time. When you go to KFC today, the way they cooked your chicken today will be the same way they will cook it after 6 months when you go there. And you love it that way. If something was to change in the taste of the chicken, you will know that something was not done well. If you report the issue, the manager is able to taste the chicken and know what was not done correctly. You know why? Because of the KFC recipe. Recipe is nothing but a list of processes that if all be observed thoroughly will produce an expected outcome.

That's what we need to fix in our businesses. Our business processes. Make your job simple. Don't be afraid. Outline your business processes clearly in a piece of paper. For your clients to receive a thoroughly cooked product or service from your company, what has to go where for what to do what for what to be like what? If you conquer this, you would have conquered a great milestone that many entrepreneurs are still battling today. The story tellers tells us that the *McDonald's* management closed the restaurant for a few months to focus on perfecting their internal processes that made sure that their customers going forward will be able to order food and receive it in the greatest quality they can master in less than just 60 seconds. After doing this, their business experienced a great boom. And guess what, happy customers keeps coming back with more other customers.

"... Focus on transactions and generating recurring business." Never lose the sight of the bottom-line of your business. Business is about making profits. I will say this again, you are not running a charity, and you are running a business. You are not in this to just breakeven or fight to meet your monthly working capital, you are in this to generate money that will generate more wealth for you and your business. The magic is not in getting into business, the magic is in staying in business. Focus on transactions. Don't be fooled by how busy you are producing or servicing, where are the transactions? Do not measure your growth by how much you have produced but how much you have sold. Sales.

Every product that you produce is produced to be sold. The process is not complete when the product is still there in your shelves, no, the process is complete when the product is in the hands of the customer and there is money in the bank. Have targets. Set up targets as to how many transactions do you want to have made by when. Go all out to meet those targets, do whatever you can. Keep your eyes on the transactions. Lastly, focus on generating recurring or repeat business. The customers will only keep coming back if they have enjoyed your products or services. Keep this in mind, most customers always have a choice. Look, you may be an entrepreneur, but you are a client or customer somewhere. And you could be one of the loyal customers of that place, tell me, why do you keep going to that place to buy that very same thing while there are many other alternatives out there? Now, think about it, why should your customers or clients stick with you for a while?

Business is about relationships. Healthy relationships. A good business relationship is premised on mutual benefit exercised through free and fair value exchange. Serve your customers well, you will see them keeping on coming. Treat each customer like he/she is the only customer you have. Focus on building a relationship. Repeat business is so beautiful, you are sure of business from your customers every single month. You have become part of their monthly budget. Like data bundles across Africa, they reflect on everyone's budget every single month. You can easily project your future profits and budget forward. This is something that is deliberately created and intentionally maintained.

There are so many things that entrepreneurs seeking to be profitable need to do. We will just share a few of them. Here is a few other things that you need to consider to start doing thoroughly as an entrepreneur in today's highly competitive and ever growing business world.

1) Be seen

Umesh Loona, one of Botswana's great real estate mogul once put up an advertorial in one of his street pole advertising boards written, *"Doing business without advertising is like winking to a girl in the dark, only you knows what you are doing but nobody else knows"*. You can't be a successful entrepreneur or business person if the people around you don't even know what you are selling, let alone that you are an entrepreneur. You need to be seen. You need to be known. Publicity sells.

A seller is someone who is out there in the market selling. That's where it matters the most. Actively participate in the daily transactions that happens in the market. I don't know about your country, but here where in Botswana where I come from, it is not a strange thing to find a business person sitting inside his/her office or shop for more than four hours *'waiting for customers'* to somehow find their way into the business. Look, you need to get out there and get customers into the business. We have already talked about this in other chapters. It shouldn't make you comfortable that there is someone in your territory who doesn't know about your business. You need to be on fire to preach about your business. Be so passionate to tirelessly talk about your business until they call you with the name of your business. Put it in their faces, always. Look, in today's times, it doesn't cost much to make noise about your business as it used to with entrepreneurs of old.

Today we have the luxury to use the technology that has been availed to us by other entrepreneurs to maximize our companies' potential. Do whatever you can to be seen. To be known. Southern Africa alone has about 65.3 million people. Did you know that instead of printing and distributing flyers which will be thrown into the next bin anyway just a few minutes after being collected, you can invest just a quarter of that budget into sponsoring posts on Facebook and reach millions of people in Southern Africa with your business. Go where the people are. The simplest and the cheapest place is social media.

Be attractive

Publicity sells. You need to understand that your image is a great commodity. We have said it before in one of the chapters of this book that entrepreneurship is about capturing and keeping customers. Look at the word *'capturing'* for a minute. Think about it. What comes to your mind when you think about that word? No one buys something that does not affect them in any way. You need to understand that there is too many of you in the market. You need to stand out. You need to be visible, far above that you have to have the pheromone that attracts customers to you. You need to have *"that thing"*. Wear the right attire. Exactly, how else were you planning to have customers flocking to your business? You can't force them.

Why is it so important for one to look attractive? For me, let me see, the first thing that got to my mind is capturing the attention of the people. Have you ever seen something attractive before? I remember my first time consciously seeing a very beautiful girl for the first time, I don't know what happened, but for some minute, I'm not sure how long it was accurately, everybody in the background blurred up, I couldn't hear anything, my heart was very heavy. She looked at me, I'm not so sure what I did, but she smiled and passed. I spent the entire month with that girl on my mind. I couldn't remember her face exactly, but I remembered accurately how she made me feel. I believe the ladies will agree with me, do you remember that shoe you saw the other time in that shop? That dress? I believe it made you feel exactly how I felt when I met this girl. I can't mention her name, for security reasons.

But let's face it, there's just something about attractive things that just gets imprinted in our hearts. First impressions. Very important. You need to give the best first impression to every client that will ever come across your product or service. Even your office, shop or even your merchandise. Be attractive. Attraction is beautiful. It compels someone to agree with the pulling force that is drawing them towards you. Attraction is always less expensive and more profitable in the long term than pushing people into your business. Radiate with beauty. Radiate with elegance. In everything.

Be reliable

Some things can't wait. Literally. I'm serious. More especially when they are considered as needs and not wants. We are living in the times where buying something is no longer only about *'how much it costs'* but also about '*how soon can I get it'*. Efficiency and reliability is paramount in today's business world. In fact, many businesses grow simply because their value proposition is premised on their ability to deliver quality within the shortest time possible and maybe for a very fair price. And guess what, this is not just something they only say with their mouths, it is something they actually do, on daily basis. They have positioned their companies in a way in which they are able to deliver with great efficiency.

You want to be predictable to your clients when it comes to their confidence with regards to exactly when they should expect their order. We used to really struggle with this reliability thing, we would promise clients that we will deliver in exactly five working days, and things gets so busy, sometimes disorganized, sometimes we just get lazy, and we would deliver even a month later. Do you know what's happening to our clients as we do this? They get impatient. We lose their trust. They begin to talk to other potential clients about their experience with our company. Before we know it, the only thing we are known for is making promises we never keep.

I had a chat with one of my friends and he said to me, *"always under-promise and over perform"*. I began to see something, the more I exceed my client's expectations is the more I win their trust. The more I win their trust is the more I create a business relationship with them, this relationship is the one that ensures that they will keep coming back to buy more from me. Generating a growing recurring income. Whenever they need me, I'm always there. I'm reliable. That's what you want to ensure that you are doing in your business. How many customers have already told you that you are not reliable? Don't take that feedback for granted, work on it. Imagine how many other customers are out there holding the same opinion about you but they never told you, it is not that they are keeping quiet about it, they are talking to other people about it.

Satisfy

Be so good with what you do that your clients can't help it but fall in love with your company. When we say *'satisfy'*, we don't mean *'reach the bare* minimum'. It is not about doing the least you could do. You are the man in this relationship, you should always find a way of going an extra mile for the client. If the relationship with your clients is more important to you then you will know that long term relationships are a series of short term relationships managed well. Client always have an option to. Anytime is tea time. Make it your habit to bring great satisfaction to your clients. It is not about having much to do great, it is about doing the best you can with the little that you have.

One of the greatest feelings in life is the feeling of satisfaction. Have you ever hoped for something good to happen, and it happens even much better than you thought it would? To those who are believers would know that God is a specialist when it comes to exceeding someone's expectations, that's why we love him. He does exceedingly, abundantly and above all that we can think or imagine. Imagine the feeling. Have you ever craved something and someone just decides to get it for you in larger quantities and proportions? And the exact same flavor you wanted? Imagine the feeling.

If you live in Africa you will know that nothing satisfies more than a glass of cold Oros when you drink immediately you get home after a long day. Or anytime you drink it. It has *"that thing"*. That's exactly how you want your clients to feel like when you deliver your products/services. You want your solution to scratch the itch. You want to make your clients to want to consume more of your products and services. You want them to keep coming back for more. The idea is not to just get into business, the idea is to stay in business. This is how you stay in business, when you deliver what you promise. Like we have already aforementioned, the idea is to over deliver. The idea is to exceed the customer's expectations. The idea is to solve the problem that we have identified in the market. The client needs to be fulfilled by your products and services. You need to give them the satisfaction they deserve from your products or services. It's called good value for money.

Be honest

One of the greatest things that are lacking in today's business world is what Jack Welch will call *candor.* Honesty. We love covering up and hoping that maybe somehow we will be able to miraculously deliver within the brackets of the client's expectation. In every relationship, communication is key. Great communication is a great thing. If there is one thing that will make you trustworthy, reliable and even attractive in the market is your honesty. Let's face the truth, it is hard to be honest. We may want to tell the truth, but the thought of how the client will react to this information makes us want to at least not say it in order to buy time to try to fix what needs to be fixed.

I used to struggle with this challenge for a very long time. I had very few clients that I really couldn't afford to lose. Every time I had to deliver their orders and I was not ready to deliver it, I would rather try to buy some time by lying to them. One lie after the other. I was the company's everything. The manager, the coach, the accountant, the secretary, the designer, and the messenger. So the job was huge for me to do it alone on time, which is why I always wanted to buy some time with small lies.

What I didn't realize is what my former landlord taught me. She said, we are human beings, we have very little things that we have control over. She said *"All I need to know is when I can get my rent money, don't lie to me, I know your struggles"* Tell your clients the truth. If you are experiencing challenges delivering the order, pick up the phone, tell your client what is going on. Rather lose your pride than a customer. Let your clients know and understand the risks involved. Charge correctly and appropriately.

One of the greatest things that will take a lot of entrepreneurs far in their entrepreneurial journey is ***transparency***. Transparency and accountability are one of the key management tools that any organization seeking to be successful and globally competitive in this era and going forward should invest towards mastering. We need to be as transparent as possible with our clients, partners, suppliers and everybody else in your business network.

Invest in excellence

Be so good with what you do that you cannot be ignored. Whatever business you are to do, if you want to be great, you need to invest in your excellence. For some of you who are already in business, if someone else was to come and serve your market more excellently than you do, what do you think will happen to your business? Look, you are already in business, what's the point of doing it substandard? Invest in excellence. Excellence is the ultimate result of the attention paid to the individual details of the whole component. Love excellence. Breathe excellence. Live excellence. Love the beauty of excellence. Commit yourself to the principle of excellence. Look, I am aware that excellence is expensive to many people. But listen, excellence is not about having everything, it is about doing the best you possibly can with the little that you have.

Most of us are just excellence away from reaching our wildest dreams in our businesses. Let excellence be seen in everything you do. From production to packaging and even in distribution. Be clothed with excellence. People love people who takes themselves seriously. There is always a better way of doing something. Some businesses around the world are only *"excellence"* away from stepping into the world of their wildest dreams. Some will pack out faster than they thought if other people moved in to their space and only offered what they are offering but more excellently. Keep on improving your solution. Just because it works now and people loves it means you should relax.

Hear this, if you are to do something for the second time for the same audience, always strive to do it even much better. Business is about giving customers new and uncommon experiences. Commit yourself to innovation. To self-improvement. You can get better at what you are doing. Some entrepreneurs are just lazy. They also know that they can do better, but they chose not to. Don't wait for a competitor to set foot in your space for you to start working harder. You can offer excellence even no one is forcing you to. You can do it. Shame on you always if you choose to do less than you know you can do. Always.

Go for the numbers

Business is in the numbers. That's the understanding that you need to get to. Without the numbers, it will never make business sense. Anything that you do in business, it doesn't matter what it is, it has to be backed by numbers. You can talk about marketing strategies that you want to use to grow your company to the regional level in two years, but here is the thing, when we look at your projections, if this statement is not reflected on those numbers, it is as good as selling dreams. You need to know the numbers and what they mean. Every entrepreneur needs to know at least the basics of accounting. Even if you don't know how to prepare the financial statements, you have to at least know or have an idea of what they mean. They were so complex to me when I saw them for the first time, but I had no choice because the business I was in was highly dependent on my knowledge of the numbers that were in those financial statements. I had no choice. Even you, for as long as you are going to be doing business in this highly competitive world in 2017 and beyond, you need to give in and subdue yourself with the knowledge of the numbers.

Like every other thing, we need to start by learning the basics. Look, entrepreneurship is about solving problems. We do this by offering solutions to the market. The first thing that you need to know is the cost that you will incur to offer such solution to the market. You need to know how much it will require you to have that solution used by your target market. You also need to know, based on your knowledge of the cost, how much mark-up are you putting on top to determine your selling price. At least have that cleared out for now. Secondly, you need to know the size of your target market, in numbers. Not just numbers, actual numbers of your target market. You need to know in percentages, the quota of that target market which you will be specifically dealing with.

Just because there are about a thousand people who could possibly use your service or product means that your target market is a thousand people. No. Of that thousand people, not all of them can afford your products or services. You need to be honest with yourself. Even though there are a thousand people that could possibly use your solution, there is nothing wrong with targeting the hundred of that one thousand who can possibly use your service or product and they can afford to pay for it. You are not a charitable entity, you are a business. Here me, imagine me saying the statement I'm about to say with a very huge microphone on top of the biggest speaker in the world: If someone can't pay, they are not your target market. I had a very big problem with accepting this truth.

Trust me, I'm not saying you can't give people your solution for free, you can, in fact, in certain occasions you should. It's called CSR/CSI. *Corporate Social Responsibility* or *Corporate Social Investment*. Sometimes you are going to have to use marketing strategies like giving people the products or services for free to penetrate the market. What I'm saying is that don't count those people as your target market, at least for now. Of course, you may not transact from them directly, but they can open doors for you to a potential customer that you will transact from. Be smart.

Understand & hedge the risks

There is an uncertainty associated with every form of business. It will be detrimental for you to get into a business with risks you are not aware of. You need to know through your SWOT analysis, the risks associated with the business you are doing. You need to be very honest with yourself about this. If there is one thing that you feel may jeopardize the future of your business you need to research more about it and be sure to do something about it. You should always talk about these worst case scenarios when you pitch your business to investors. Risk is not meant to be known and accepted. It is meant for you as the entrepreneur to make up your mind to find ways in which you are going to hedge these risks. Some situations may be beyond your control, sometimes they may not entirely be beyond your control.

You have to seat down with your team and research about how the events of these worst case scenarios may unfold and see how you can plan ahead to hedge these risks before they happen. Instead of losing 40%, what can you do to reduce these losses to at least 20%. It is the same as the banks, when you apply for their loans, they will always want to secure their loan that they are giving to you with what they call collateral. Normally it will be a piece of land or any form of assets that belongs to you. If your business is that good, why should the banks still want to secure their loan? Here is the truth, no matter how many times we have calculated the risks using countless methods, things sometimes pens out the way we least expected.

It is always best at all times that we become acutely aware of the risks we are exposed to. When we launch a new product/service, or we are hiring, or purchasing an asset, firing someone, partnering with another person or organization, or even getting into business in the first place. I have to say this, the fact that there is a risk you could be possibly exposed to doesn't means that you should abort the mission. We are different. We have different risk appetites. Some people believe in the higher powers of the supreme beings, and because of that their faith allows them to leverage on their risks and pursue without reservation. It is entirely up to you. I normally say that if the return on your sacrifice is smaller than the sacrifice itself, don't risk the sacrifice. Personally, I risk everything I have if what I'm likely to get is bigger than what I'm sacrificing or equals to it. Some people risks in percentages, they are willing to sacrifice this much only if their worst case scenario losses are not bigger than a certain percentage.

Speak the language

The biggest favor you can ever do to yourself in your business life is learning how to speak the business language. Every profession has a language. The doctors have their own language. The programmers also have their language. The police. The defense force. The taxi drivers, everybody has a language. Similarly, the business world also has a way in which it communicates in a way in which it will make sense to the business people. Of course I don't mean language like there is English, Spanish or Setswana. I'm referring to the terminologies and phrases that are commonly used by top business people. You don't want to sound like a 'civilian' when you speak to business people. The language is used in many occasions, some of which you will be discussing deals and many other things. What's detrimental to you is not the fact that you may seem too unschooled in the language, but the fact that you will be too vulnerable to fall victim should you come in contact with people who use this language to manipulate others in business.

Just like almost every other language, the business language can be learnt. It can be mastered. It can be taught. We learn word by word. When we listen to those who are fluent in it, through passion and curiosity, we can grasp a lot in a short space of time. That's the main thing there, we need to expose ourselves to environments and platforms where this language is spoken. In this world of endless possibilities and abundant resources, the internet world, it is even much easier to learn without even stepping a foot in a physical school. I can personally attest to this that I am who I am today mainly because of my own personal development. Thanks to the internet. I learnt and tested until I was a pro in what I was learning.

I honestly believe that the more you allow yourself to be exposed to seminars, workshops, webinars, documentaries and business movies, you will most definitely improve in your understanding of the business language. There are several commonly used terminologies and phrases which I think you need to find time and school yourself in. Just like you start by learning that the Setswana word for *'hello'* is *'dumela',* you start there. The basics. When you talk to people like investors or banks, they expect you to be at a certain level of understanding of at least the basics. They expect you to at least know the basic business terms. Not that they are going to give you an examination on 'business terms', No, but in your conversation you have to sound like the man or the woman they are looking for. The person who is speaking their language.

Every business industry or career path has its own language. Every industry in the world has its own terms that it uses to communicate the concepts, processes and many other things that makes out that specific industry. You have to give yourself to the learning and mastering of that language. You have be proficient in it. Speak like the people from your industry. Be informed about the new things that comes into your industry. Research about the new trends in your line of business. What will be happening when in your industry? You have to know these things. Be confident in the language used in your industry. I used to be shy to speak like business people. Sometimes I will be in a workshop and people will be throwing in different acronyms and big terms I had no idea what they were talking about. I will feel out of place. But I was eager to learn what those things mean.

I remember one night I didn't sleep, I had heard some young lady during the day in a meeting we were attending where we were advising *Botswana Government* on what needs to be done to create a new tertiary education financing solution, the lady said *"we need to find a holistic approach",* look, this doesn't sound like a big term but it was to me because I was hearing it for the first time at 18 years old by then. I didn't sleep, I was bothered, *"what is a holistic approach?",* until I found out. I was so happy a few weeks later because I could confidently use the word and others that I learnt. Since then, I learnt to research about every term, every concept, every name and everything I hear being mentioned in my industry that I didn't know about.

Persuade

Let me ask you this, what is the greatest skill that entrepreneurs must have? It is being creative to solve problems, right? WRONG. The greatest skill entrepreneurs must have in them is the ability to sell. We have talked about this in the previous chapters. You need to know how to sell. You can't say you will get someone to do that for you. You have to know how to do it yourself. You need to practice sales until you become really good with it. I once gave some of our Project124 participants an assignment, I said to them, *"go to the streets and get 300 people to say NO to your products or services".* They looked at me and they said *'we should get No(s), why not yes?'* The answer was simple, it is easy to get a NO when you are looking for a YES. The inverse is also true. The more you talk to people about your products and services in your quest to sell to them, the more you get refined to become more persuasive. The more you do it the more you will learn different market segments that are there, this will help you to define your target market better.

You cannot sell if you can't persuade. You cannot sign some deals if you can't persuade. You can't move certain things in your business if you can't persuade. Persuasion is not only about following people up, I'm talking about your ability to persuade someone with your words. The ability to persuade someone with your charisma. The ability to force people to consider buying your products and services even when they were planning not to without the use of violence but the force of inspiration.

People need to feel persuaded to follow you. People need to feel persuaded to represent your products and services. People need to feel persuaded to make your business a part of their life. People need to feel persuaded to associate with you because your school of thought makes them feel inspired. Learn to persuade. Learn to pitch in a persuasive manner. Learn to speak in a persuasive manner. Own the show when you speak. Own the moment when you present. Let your products and services standout when they are put with the rest. When you name a business or a product, persuade. When you create a tagline for your billboard or any form of advertorial, persuade.

Let people be hooked and convicted by anything that represent you. You can do this. Just learn how to do it. You cannot afford to exist in today's business world without mastering the art of persuasion. Learn it and be good with it.

Do you remember when you first saw this book? Oh yes, your mind was running around the city trying to believe what you are seeing. Here is the fact, you may not have agreed with the tittle, but you still bought the copy anyway. And you are still reading it. Look at you, you are even on page 166. Persuasion. That's what I want you to do to your customers. Persuade them. Grab their attention.

CHAPTER 28

DON'T DIE WITH YOUR DREAM

"The tragedy of life is not death but what we let die inside us while we live"

- Norman Cousins

There are hundreds, millions and billions of solutions to the world's greatest challenges that hasn't been discovered yet, one of them is in you. What are you planning to do with it? How long should we wait to see you doing it? The world is waiting, Africa is waiting. It has been waiting ever since you were born. And it is waiting for that day when their problems will be over. Lives are depending on the success of your idea. You are not just dreaming, you are seeing possibilities of a better future. Dreams are possibilities, one has to believe and act on them because their actualization is the liberation of the many. We are where we are today in the world because of the realization of other people's dreams, the world will be where it will be in the future because of the realization of our dreams.

It would have been an error if innovation would have stopped with the Nokia 3310, it will still be an error if innovation will stop with the iPhone X and the Huawei P10 or Samsung Galaxy S8. One day young people around the world will laugh that I was talking about this models of mobile phones as the latest inventions of our time, and they will be shocked to find out that we thought this models were awesome devices with cutting edge technologies. It would have been an error if Mark Zuckerberg didn't act on his dream of connecting the world through revolutionizing social media. One greatest man that ever lived by the name Dr. Myles Munroe once said, *"the wealthiest place on earth is not the gold mines of South Africa or the oil mines of North Africa, the wealthiest place on earth is the cemetery, because buried there are businesses that were never opened, books that were never published, music we never heard, movies we never saw, cars we never drove, buildings we never saw and champions we never celebrated".*

Imagine yourself lying on the grave with your idea that was meant to save millions of lives and destinies, given to you by God, trusting the ability he has put on you, the resources he put around you and the challenges he allowed you to go through. There are lives counting on the success of your idea, there are lives counting on your dream, disappoint the grave, ***"don't die with your dream, launch it".***

MESSAGE FROM THE AUTHOR

"Thank you very much for buying this book. By buying this book, you were not only investing in your own growth as an entrepreneur, you were also investing in building a platform that will develop globally competitive entrepreneurs in Africa and connect them with businesses and markets around the world. It will take significant amount of money to finish this project, and your contribution has made a huge difference. I wish above all things that you may prosper as your business prospers. May God bless you and may God bless Africa."

- Goitsemang J. Khutsafalo (Author)

Goitsemang J. Khutsafalo is an internationally renowned author, serial disruptor at heart, entrepreneur and empowerment expert. The author of 'Think like an Entrepreneur, Act like a Prostitute'. He has been listed on the 'Top twenty most inspirational youth in Botswana 2013". He is the Founding President of All Brilliant Minds Organization (ALBRIMO) and also the Founder and Managing Director of Launchit International (Pty) Ltd which owns and manages the Project124 Entrepreneurship program as well as the Pioneers Megafest. He has over six years of experience working directly with communities and young people focusing on entrepreneurship, innovation and education development and empowerment of youth in Botswana. He is passionate about building a globally competitive entrepreneurship culture and entrepreneurs in Africa.

think like an entrepreneur, act like a prostitute

In today's business world, it is not about what you are selling but how you are selling it that matters the most. We are blessed to be alive today during this amazing time, the best time ever in the history of history to be an entrepreneur. The first time I received this title in my mind, I was flabbergasted for many days. I got very curious, it sounded very captivating. This book carries insights, wisdom and power to transposition you into a globally competitive entrepreneur.

It is time to shake the world. It doesn't matter which part of the world you are coming from or what you have been going through, we exist at a very precious time on earth, the only time on earth where you could be somewhere deep in the village but able to build something that can shake the world and change lives of people around the world. The only time where doing business even across the incarceration of your boarders doesn't even require you to live the comfort of your own house. We are blessed to be alive in the world where all these are not just possibilities but realities that we already see happening around us. It is now time for it to happen to us.

By buying this book, you are not only just investing into your own growth as an entrepreneur, you are also investing into a vision that will transform entrepreneurship development in Africa. A vision that will make it possible for African entrepreneurs to hit the global markets with their home grown businesses. The author therefore requests you to partner with him in this vision to develop the quality of entrepreneurship in Africa.

It is time to do entrepreneurship differently. You are therefore invited to a higher dimension, a new level of function, thought, competence and performance. You want to be successful in your business? Think like an entrepreneur, and act like a prostitute.

GET IN TOUCH WITH US

@JKhuts Goitsemang J. Khutsafalo GJKhutsafalo

GJK

Goitsemang J. Khutsafalo

ISBN: 978-99968-0-668-1

EAN

9 789996 806681